Kristin Ohlson, a free[...]ction writer, has been publish[...] *Ms. Magazine, O: The Oprah [...], Discover, The New Scientist, Food & Wine, Tin House, Poets & Writers,* and many other publications. A teacher, she occasionally works with creative writing students at Cleveland State University and women prisoners at the Cuyahoga County jail. A recipient of the Ohio Art Council's Individual Artists Fellowship in Fiction for 2003–2004, she lives in Cleveland, Ohio.

Stalking the Divine

Kristin Ohlson

A PLUME BOOK

PLUME
Published by Penguin Group
Penguin Group (USA) Inc., 375 Hudson Street, New York, New York 10014, U.S.A.
Penguin Group (Canada), 10 Alcorn Avenue, Toronto, Ontario, Canada M4V 3B2
(a division of Pearson Penguin Canada Inc.)
Penguin Books Ltd, 80 Strand, London WC2R 0RL, England
Penguin Ireland, 25 St Stephen's Green, Dublin 2, Ireland (a division of Penguin Books Ltd)
Penguin Group (Australia), 250 Camberwell Road, Camberwell, Victoria 3124, Australia
(a division of Pearson Australia Group Pty Ltd)
Penguin Books India Pvt Ltd, 11 Community Centre, Panchsheel Park,
New Delhi - 110 017, India
Penguin Books (NZ), Cnr Airborne and Rosedale Roads, Albany, Auckland 1310, New Zealand
(a division of Pearson New Zealand Ltd)
Penguin Books (South Africa) (Pty) Ltd, 24 Sturdee Avenue, Rosebank, Johannesburg 2196,
South Africa

Penguin Books Ltd, Registered Offices: 80 Strand, London WC2R 0RL, England

Published by Plume, a member of Penguin Group (USA) Inc. This is an authorized reprint of a
hardcover edition published by Hyperion. For information address Hyperion, 77 West 66th Street,
New York, New York 10023-6298.

First Plume Printing, January 2005
10 9 8 7 6 5 4 3 2 1

 REGISTERED TRADEMARK-MARCA REGISTRADA

The Library of Congress has catalogued the Hyperion edition as follows:
Ohlson, Kristin
Stalking the divine : contemplating faith with the Poor
Clares / Kristin Ohlson.—1st ed.
p. cm.
ISBN 1-4013-0025-1 (hc.)
ISBN 0-452-28640-9 (pbk.)
1. Adoration Monastery (Cleveland, Ohio). 2. Poor
Clares—Ohio—Cleveland—Spiritual life. 3. Ohlson,
Kristin, 1951—Religion. I. Title.
BX4364.C57O45 2003
255'.973—dc21   2002192178

Printed in the United States of America

In memory of my father,
Louis Ohlson,
an uncommonly good man
1912–2003

Acknowledgments

Many thanks to the Poor Clares of Perpetual Adoration for allowing me to peer into their lives and use their experience to try to grasp this slippery matter of faith: they received my questions with grace, humor, and tremendous kindness. Thanks also to the wonderful priests associated with St. Paul Shrine—Senan Glass, Bob Marva, and Mick Joyce—who encouraged my pursuit. And thanks to the others who offered their time, expertise, and wisdom, including Tim Barrett, Marietta Starrie, Mary Rose Kocab, Chris Krosel, Don Petit, James Mannion, Carol Poh Miller, Maureen Kreick, Andrew Peter Thompson, and unnamed others. I am grateful to you all.

Thanks to Marly Rusoff, my agent, and Leigh Haber, my editor—how glad I am to have found you!

I'm also grateful to the friends and family who cheered me on as I wrote this book. I'm lucky to have four great families—Ohlsons, Metzkers, Blumbergs, and Stanleys—as well as great friends. Special thanks to Susan Lubell, Linda Miller, Skip

Harger, my pals and teachers from the Bennington Writing Seminars, and Mary Grimm and Susan Grimm Dumbrys: the Grimm sisters' writing camaraderie has bolstered and buoyed me for years. Thanks finally to Matt, Jamie Rose, and JD, blessings all.

Stalking the Divine

1

I t was my fifth Christmas morning without my two children. Their father and I had agreed after our divorce that Jamie and Matthew would spend this holiday with him—a day always ribboned with loveliness and impossible yearning and melancholy, but the latter had taken over. Without the children, I was desperate for joy, so desperate that I decided to go to church.

As I unfolded the morning paper, I imagined the kids still sleeping, not wanting to wake up to the absence of their childhood and the ghosts of family Christmases past. Then I imagined them up and about, groggily partaking in some holiday routine that had developed without me, a new collection of small observances they'd no doubt accumulated during their last four Christmases. There would be no stockings to tug away from the hearth, no little feet scurrying to see what Santa might have left them—after all, they were both in their early twenties, and their father is Jewish and didn't go in for as much Christmas frippery as he did when the two of us were together. Still, I

brooded over sentimental tableaus featuring the four of them—
the kids, my ex-husband, and his then-fiancée—without me.
Did they have a special breakfast together while listening to
Bing Crosby sing "White Christmas"? Did they go for an early
walk in the woods and hang up strings of popcorn for the
chickadees? Did they put together a box of winter gloves for
families at a homeless shelter? Had an altogether more festive
and wholesome holiday regimen flowered in my absence? Or
did the children bicker with their father and grumble about getting up before noon and snipe at his fiancée? In a gratifyingly
selfish way, I enjoyed that tableau the most.

The children had spent Christmas Eve at my house, the
house that still bears all the scars from their childhood, with my
new husband, JD, and me. We opened our presents and threw
balled-up wrapping paper at the dog. My daughter and I played
the sound track to *Footloose* over and over again and danced
around the dining room table, while my husband and son
watched an old movie. Now, my husband and I were alone in
the bleakness of Christmas morning. My children had left at
around midnight, and my husband's teenaged boys wouldn't
arrive from Florida until the next day. Even though we'd been
adopted by friends for Christmas dinner those last few years,
there were still many long, dead hours to endure before the holiday lights would start to shine again in our house.

As I paged idly through the newspaper looking for after-
Christmas sales, I stumbled upon a section about local religious
activities, including a full page of boxed ads for Christmas services. "Have churches always advertised?" I said out loud, but
only the dog was in the room to hear me, and she just sighed.

When I was a child, there didn't seem to be a need for advertisements soliciting churchgoers: going to mass was not a choice but an obligation, and families packed the pews so tightly that the lint from one thigh passed to another. Churches didn't have to put announcements in the paper to tell people the times of the masses and the name of the pastor. Back in Oroville, my little California hometown, there was only one Catholic church—St. Thomas—and my family and its regulars knew the schedule. Not many strangers came around, so there was never a need to announce such things. Cleveland has always had hundreds of churches, dozens of them Catholic. Maybe, I thought, the various congregations have always had a greater need to distinguish themselves from each other.

In any case, churches advertise now. In the weeks leading up to Christmas, I had seen many ads. Just as restaurants advertised holiday meals in *The Plain Dealer*'s food section, just as theaters and community centers advertised Christmas shows and pageants in the entertainment section, many of Cleveland's churches placed boxed ads in the Saturday paper or in flyers stuffed in my mailbox. Some offered special Christmas services with live animals that children could feed and fondle. Some had live nativity scenes, with actors dressed as Mary, Joseph, shepherds, and wise men, with real squalling babies standing in for Jesus. Many offered carols and candlelight.

The last Christmas service I'd attended was in 1993, the year of my first miserable Christmas without my kids, and it was a date. There were carols and candlelight, but I wasn't interested in communion with the many or even with God; I was only burning for intimacy with JD, whom I had just met. On our first date, we went out for dinner at my favorite restaurant, found we couldn't eat the glass noodles and shrimp because we'd spoiled our appetites just looking at each other, then went out dancing at a blues bar. I felt the heat of his hand on my back for days. On our second date, we went to my friend Mary's Christmas party. We both smoked a cigarette, and my fingers were so moist they left prints on the filter; he held an ashtray in his palm for me, and Mary and I whispered about him. On our third date, we went downtown to the Christmas Eve midnight service at the Old Stone Church on Public Square. We dashed through empty streets toward the church, its stained-glass windows glowing in the dark, running as the millions of stars became bright beads of snow in our hair and the wind from Lake Erie blew up our sleeves. Inside the church, there were hundreds of candles, the romance of faith lit with tiny flames. The choir sang mightily and we held hands, so nervous with each other that our fingers shook. The minister disappointed me, however, delivering some stock sermon about truth or goodness or beauty. Just as new lovers discount the flaws that they surely see in each other, I decided to ignore the din of his platitudes in JD's and my otherwise rapturous night. In any case, it was less an occasion of faith than of lust.

Five years later, it was 1998, a half year after we had been married: I wanted to go to Christmas services, and I wanted to go alone. I knew by now that even though JD would come with me if I asked, this was my longing, not his. The previous year, I had made my annual checklist of things I wanted to accomplish in the coming months, and sidling up to faith, as usual, was one of them—it had been on the list for several years, along with lifting weights and reading Proust. A few days before Christmas, I reviewed my list and shook my head at the things not done; I said, "Oh no, I forgot to believe in God!" mocking my own foolishness for putting faith on the same list with reupholstering Aunt Leah's rocking chair. I had worked a little at the faith thing during the past year, but my sorties were few and unpromising. I'd gone to one lovely old church for a few weeks, but then the priest railed about abortion and homosexuality one Sunday and I knew his wasn't a universe I could fit into. Besides, that church was located in an Italian neighborhood famous for toughs who were known to jump black people as they passed through. I'm not black, but still, I kept looking at the faces around me and wondering if they would be so keen to share a pew with me if I were. Being in that church reminded me of my seventeenth summer, when I lived with a family in Austria—I'd eye the faces of the friendly villagers and wonder where they'd stood when the Nazis were killing the Jews. The other churches I visited didn't hold me either: too fancy or too plain, with priests who were too perfunctory or too arrogant or just too dull for my tastes.

Picky, picky. Still, as I looked through the newspaper and checked out the services described in all those little boxes, I realized I now had simpler expectations. On this lonely day, I wanted to be surrounded by the rituals of the faith I had grown up with and then bolted from as a teenager. I wanted to be in the midst of people who had gathered to share a belief in something greater than the assorted daily struggles of their lives. I wanted to sing and bow and kneel and pray along with them. Even if I didn't share their convictions, I thought it possible to be infected by their fervor, to pick up a tiny germ of faith that might quicken and grow. Why this longing, why now? I wanted a steadying hope after my twenty-two-year marriage had ended, after this new one had begun, after my children had the audacity to grow up and my parents the audacity to grow old, after I had sensed that whatever I thought I knew of the world wasn't enough. During most of my life I had considered faith a kind of sickness, something that softened the brain and allowed the soothing delusion of divine power. Now I wanted faith, but I wasn't sure if I hadn't inoculated myself against it for good.

At the bottom of the page, one box finally held my attention. It described a Christmas mass at St. Paul Shrine, a downtown church I hadn't heard of before in a neighborhood that used to be one of the wealthiest in the nation and still has a few magnificent buildings amid the urban dissolution. There was only one service, at 11:30 in the morning, which meant there was still time enough for me to find my way there and even to arrive with clean hair. Franciscan priests would say mass, the ad stated, and nuns from an order called the Poor Clares of Perpetual Adoration would sing. I had fond, storybook images of Franciscans with doves on their shoulders and fawns eating from their hands. I had never heard of the Poor Clares—they sounded a little like something from a *Saturday Night Live* skit— but I liked the mysterious pathos of their name. This was the box I ripped from the paper.

After talking on the phone to my kids—who found my going to mass as unlikely and alarming as if I were off to a seance—and kissing my husband good-bye, I left the snow-felted lawns and garlanded porches of Cleveland Heights and drove downtown. Cleveland's downtown streets are even lonelier on Christmas Day than they are at night. They were especially bleak that morning, crusted in places with dirty snow and ashen in others where the road salt had eaten away the ice. When I arrived at St. Paul Shrine a few minutes early, I realized that I had driven past it perhaps a hundred times without noticing it. In this once-posh stretch of Euclid Avenue some forty blocks from Public Square, I had always been more interested in a dim sum restaurant around the block, the secondhand store up the street, a decaying building at the corner that had been the site of some ancient rock-and-roll event, the soot-blackened Masonic auditorium nearby, the big old tree that once caught a few dozen plastic bags in its branches and fluttered them like laundry for a month. I don't know why this multispired hulk hadn't caught my notice before—maybe just because there are a lot of big old churches in Cleveland, and it doesn't look a thing like the little brick church I'd attended back in Oroville.

There was so little traffic near St. Paul that I was able to make a big swooping U-turn on Euclid Avenue and park right in front of the church. In fact, there was so little traffic that I had to consult the newspaper clipping in my pocket to make sure I had the right time. No one else seemed to be going in, but I followed a trail of rock salt to one of the doors—at least someone had been out that morning to make sure no one slipped and fell on the ice—and assumed there must be a parking lot on the other side of the church that the regulars used. Inside the dimly lit church lobby, I hesitated a minute to look at the bulletin boards with curling notices of meetings and special collections, at a statue of Mary with wires pointing toward her son where two plaster fingers had broken off, at the three sets of dark wooden doors in front of me. I entered through the doors on the left, uneasy about walking into the middle of things.

Inside, nothing about St. Paul Shrine met my expectations.

As my eyes adjusted to the dark and I sat down in a pew at the back, I began to make out marble angels bending toward the altar, so white and sinuously chiseled they looked like porcelain. I saw paintings of lilies, passion flowers, wheat, and ivy curling along the high gold-colored wall over the altar; carved wooden panels like dense, brown lace that stretched across the front of the church, making a deep, square indentation around the back of the altar; thick columns with cornices of molded flowers with studded stems and dusky red tongues; windows where biblical stories were told in heavy chunks of glass the color of jewels. I tipped back my head and saw that the ceiling was also a gallery of images, painted flowers and symbols boxed into heavy wooden molding, then wide leaping arches painted in turquoise, coral, and amber. The church was incredibly beautiful, detailed in delicate ways that belied its heavy stone exterior. I felt as if I had walked into a Fabergé box.

My first surprise was that I could have turned in circles for the entire service and continued finding things to admire. The second was that I could have turned in circles with my arms stretched wide and whirled up and down the length of the pew without bumping into anyone: the church was nearly empty. I recalled something about the Marriage of Canaan, something about many being called and few being chosen. Here, it seemed to be a little different: St. Paul had called many through their newspaper ad, but few had chosen to come. I looked around the dimly lit church. Where were all the holiday worshipers? I wondered. Where were the Poor Clares of Perpetual Adoration, whispering their prayers in the semidarkness and moistening their lips for the carols that would remind the faithful of the choirs of angels attending Jesus' birth? I saw a solitary pianist at the front of the church, the knot of his tie illuminated by a desk lamp. I saw another thirty or so congregants, not gathered together but dispersed so that no more than one or two sat in a pew. As the time for mass approached, a few more people came in and claimed their stretches of empty space. I assumed that the Poor Clares would make a formal entrance and fill the first two rows of pews, but a man with a torn and stained coat was the only person who sat in the front row. The second, and perhaps the third and fourth, remained empty.

Finally, the overhead lights came on to announce the beginning of the service. A silver-haired and bearded priest entered from a room behind the carved wooden panels at the right of the altar. He wasn't followed by peach-fuzzed altar boys in lace smocks—this was how I had remembered the mass, the way I thought it would always look. Instead, he was attended by another man nearly as old and worn as himself. Still, the face the priest turned to the congregation was jubilant and welcoming. From way in the back, it was hard to hear him, but the few phrases I caught sounded good to me—kindly and smart and freshly thought through, as if he had just finished scribbling his notes behind the wooden panel. He stumbled over a few of his words, and I even liked that; I felt it showed an unrehearsed sincerity. I consulted one of the daily programs lying on the pew and figured that he must be Father Senan Glass, St. Paul's pastor.

The Poor Clares were nowhere in sight, and it seemed that the mass would commence without them. But as the pianist spread out his sheets of music and began to play, human voices joined him—not the disparate voices of those of us in the pews, but a cluster of voices from behind the carved wooden panels to the left of the altar. I leaned forward, eyes half closed, waiting for the voices to soar and lift my soul into the rafters, where it might hover around the painted likeness of St. Paul. But my eyes opened again as I realized these were the voices of mere women, many of whom sounded old and frail, who faltered over the notes and struggled with the tempo, even as the pianist lifted a hand from his chords every now and then to gesture rhythmically toward their hidden struggle with the music. I wondered when they would enter the church. Then the singing stopped and the priest resumed the mass, but the choir of nuns did not march inside. I realized that the Poor Clares must be cloistered—cloistered nuns in this day and age!—thus the shelter of the carved panels, thus the voices that sounded as if they were used only on rare occasions. I leaned forward to look more closely at their enclosure and saw that there was a horizontal section on the side facing the altar where the heavy carving had been removed, leaving a more open fretwork of turned wood. I could see the nuns there, dark bowed shapes and an occasional pale, upturned face.

I found all this fascinating, though in a sort of detached way. I was already fashioning the story into one of ironic amusement for my family and friends: the nuns who sang like sparrows when I had expected angels, the altar boys given way to altar geezers, the odd and plaintive and sometimes decidedly one-note-short-of-an-octave voices I could hear from the pews around me. I relished the artwork at St. Paul but was untouched by the spirit that had inspired it. As with the other churches I had visited, I assumed that I probably wouldn't come back.

Suddenly a shift, a jolt, a rupture from irony. From the beginning of the service, I had been aware of an older man sitting in the pew behind me. I'd figured he was just another stranger who had slipped in to warm himself with this proximity to the holiday faithful. Since his clothes were worn and drab, since he was sitting at the very back of the church, possibly also since he was black and I am white, I had made an instant judgment—the kind you're hardly even aware of—that he might be homeless and need the actual warmth of the building itself. As the mass continued, I was aware of his movements just a few feet behind me, imagined that the draft against my neck was his breath, and I wished I were sitting in the middle of an even greater gap of space. Then I heard him stumble to his feet and rustle around; I turned to see him picking up the collection baskets at the back of the church. A few other people stood at his cue, and he limped toward them, handed out the baskets, and they began to take a collection. I winced at my suburban snottiness, at my hastening to judgment: I had assumed he was one of the needy, but instead he was one of the givers.

I dutifully pulled out my checkbook. There were many envelopes lying on the pew, earmarking donations for the St. Paul Restoration Fund, the flower fund, the utilities fund, the candle fund, daily meals for the hungry, and a few others. This church needed so much, I thought, and I considered putting a small amount in each envelope. Instead, I put a check for ten dollars in the meal fund envelope and dropped it in a basket when it came my way.

But there was more to this ritual of collection than I had thought. When the man with the limp had dispatched the other collectors to their seats, he stood at the back of the church looking around, then tapped the shoulders of two women dressed in bright red coats and whispered something to them. They looked startled but got to their feet, and he gave a chalice to one and a decanter of wine to the other. He looked on my side of the aisle for a second, then settled his gaze on me and leaned over to speak. "Please take this up to Father," he said, holding one of the half-loaded collection baskets out to me. His skin was lighter in spots where it seemed that life might have pressed against him with too much force.

"To *that* Father?" I whispered back in dismay and pointed to the front of the church. "Right now?"

He nodded and shifted his weight from his bad leg.

"But I don't know what to do."

He extended his hand toward the other women, who stood in the aisle waiting for me. "I'll be right behind you," he said pleasantly, giving the basket a little shake.

I didn't think it would be polite to insist that he had tapped the wrong person: a stranger, a nonbeliever at worst, a wan believer at best, a drifter hoping to glean bits of other people's joy on this day. So I went along with him, being careful not to trip over the kneeler as I clambered up, to keep step with the two other women as we passed one dark and empty pew after another, and to keep my head up as the altar got closer. Father Senan watched our halting procession. I'm sure I must have looked as if I was marching toward a public whipping. As we reached the altar, I fumbled with the basket and tried to mimic the solemn choreography of the other two women, then handed the collection of offerings to the silver-haired priest.

"Surprised?" he asked me, chuckling a little as he removed the basket from my hands. He had a delighted smile and merry eyes, and seemed to be enjoying my dry-mouthed bemusement. Far from being a somber ascetic, he looked like an aging folk singer, one who had spent a lifetime translating passion and good cheer into song. He thanked me and the others for the offering, and as he turned back to the altar, I spied his pointed brown monk's cowl hanging down the back of his silken vestments. It was a reassuring reminder of doves and fawns.

I was both charmed and startled: in the thirty-plus years since I'd been a diligent Catholic, had it become common for priests to tease people in the middle of mass? And not just any mass, but Christmas mass? Suddenly I had found an appealing face to put on faith. If not for that moment, I might never have returned to St. Paul.

But I did return the following Sunday and the one after that, each time sitting in a different part of the church so that I could watch what was happening from a new vantage point. The progression of the mass didn't get any clearer for me, and I still didn't know what to say or do at any given point. My memories of the Latin masses of my childhood were no help. The all-English modern mass seemed to bear no relation to them, and I kept wondering where "Mea culpa, mea culpa, mea maxima culpa" belonged. People also did things in this church that had never been part of my experience, nor were they like anything I'd seen more recently in my father's or brothers' churches. When they said the Lord's Prayer, some people would hold their hands out, palms up, fingers slightly curled; sometimes they'd reach out over the pews and link their upturned hands together, like slender chains of supplication that burst apart as the prayer concluded. I wanted to know why they did this, but still felt too removed to ask. Every time the congregants went up to the altar for communion and then thoughtfully mouthed the communion host as they headed back to their seats, I'd search their faces but couldn't find anyone like myself among them. I felt that none of them could understand what I was looking for at St. Paul. I didn't even know what I was looking for.

After my first month regularly attending mass at St. Paul, I called my sister out in California and told her that I was trying out church.

"Sure," she said. "You were always the holy one."

Me? Me, the former radical communist atheist who'd taught her children to believe that belief in God is as fanciful as a belief in fairies but far more insidious? Me, whose children worried that my new interest in church might be evidence of an impending breakdown?

"Yes, you," my sister said. "We were laughing at your expense the other night. Mom and Dad pulled out a box of old photos and papers. There were a bunch of letters you wrote in second grade, going on and on about angels."

"The nuns made me do it!" I replied.

But yes, I remembered a few times in those early years when I'd felt rapturously happy in church. It was very much like the drifting-out-of-your-skin ecstasy that I later felt at political rallies, or when I was falling in love, or when holding my children in my arms. I wondered if I was going to church because I imagined this kind of heated exuberance could happen to me again. And did I even want to be that kind of believer?

After that first month, I began to recognize a few of the St. Paul regulars from a distance. Some of them looked well suited and stylish, as if they had just driven their SUVs in from the suburbs, while others looked broken and dusty, as if they'd spent the night sleeping under a bridge. There was the woman with foreboding eyebrows who always sat by the confessionals, the tweedy couple who whispered to each other throughout the service, the woman who always wore a ski hat, sneakers, and a cross the size of a potato masher around her neck. During the part of the mass when the congregants were supposed to turn and greet each other, some people had to stretch over empty pews to shake hands but the potato-masher-cross lady blew kisses at me instead. At the end of each mass, she often walked up to the front of the church and also blew kisses into the Poor Clares' enclosure.

I began to wonder what kept these faithful few coming to St. Paul Shrine and what fueled the aging cadre of priests who maintained this church. I found myself wanting to ambush them all in the church lobby and ask why these two-thousand-year-old stories meant so much to them, to demand that they explain how belief is even possible. I was especially intrigued by the Poor Clares. As I watched them disappear from view every Sunday, I wanted to drift behind them like vapor, swirling invisibly in their wake as they led a life so dedicated to—to the pursuit of God? to the pleasures of God? I wanted to watch them as they sliced apples or searched for the cord to the curtains or swung their feet to the floor after a night full of dreams. Did all these ordinary moments have greater meaning because of their faith? Was their faith more powerful because it was compressed between the walls of their monastery? How had they converted from ordinary women to these hidden brides of Christ? I knew I couldn't vaporize, but still, I wanted to tag along with them like a little kid asking why, why, why?

And then I had an idea: I would write about them. They might be willing to take time from their mysterious lives if they knew I might use their words to create a book. I had interviewed enough people for magazine articles to know that sometimes questions aren't even necessary: often, people tell me things I wouldn't even think of asking. There's an odd, exhilarating intimacy that forms during an interview—a pleasantly safe intimacy, too, as I get to ask all the questions and it's very rare that someone tries to probe me. People who like to write generally do so because it gives them a way to explore and understand things, whether these things are out in the world, buried in the vault of their own memory, or have sprung unbidden from their imagination. In my case, writing about St. Paul Shrine might help me construct a framework for trying to make sense of their faith and, perhaps, learn to build some kind of faith of my own. I sent a letter to Father Senan and told him I wanted to write about St. Paul Shrine—the building, the Poor Clares, the Franciscans, the congregation, the whole package. I acknowledged that much of my interest was personal, that I was a long-estranged Catholic with a wistfulness for faith. I told him that I wanted to discover what there was to learn about faith from those who had never left it in the first place, that I wanted to explore whether someone who had walked away from belief might find it again. And I told him that I thought there were many people like me.

A week after I sent the letter, I called Father Senan, drumming my fingers on my desk as I waited for him to come to the phone. He had promptly passed my letter on to the Poor Clares, he told me; it would be their decision since they were the ones who actually owned the church. Then he rattled off bits of history: that St. Paul had been built by the Episcopalians in 1875 and sold to a Catholic bishop in 1930, who gave it to the Poor Clares for their work. That the church used to be jammed with believers before the surrounding apartment buildings and hotels had been torn down and the land turned into parking lots. That the church used to hold a special 2:00 A.M. mass for the newspaper printers, who would shoot up to the shrine right after they put the Sunday paper into the distribution trucks, then go home and sleep until noon.

"We don't get crowds like that anymore," he said pleasantly, sounding as unfazed as if I'd asked him about a slight wilting of the lilies someone had placed around the altar. He explained that there were now less than fifty people in the congregation—no more middle-of-the-night masses, no more hordes of believers stopping by after work. And the church itself began to present a different visage—a bolted door—to visitors after the riots of the 1960s took place, as there were incidents right outside the church and the Poor Clares became frightened. The priest sighed. "The shrine always used to be open."

"What do you think of my idea?" I asked.

"Writing a book? That's a fine idea. Maybe it would bring a little money into the church. You know, I'm trying to restore the place before I leave."

"When are you leaving?" I was instantly mournful that this high-spirited holy man might be going away.

"Either after the millennium or Armageddon, whichever comes first." He chuckled lightly, promising to ask the Poor Clares about my letter.

I waited for the sisters' reply and, in the meantime, I kept going to church. Now that I'd become acquainted with Father Senan, I always stopped to say hello on my way out. He'd grip my hand and smile with such delight that I worried he was already counting me among his flock of believers. Then I noticed he was delighted by every face, from regulars like the woman with the heavy eyebrows to strays like me. If I hung around the lobby long enough, I'd get to see him disappear into the church and reemerge in his long brown Franciscan robe. I was foolishly pleased by this sight, as if I had time-traveled into the Middle Ages and was face-to-face with Friar Tuck. I had to remind myself that Father Senan's life might be as blandly modern as mine—that he probably surfed the Web and picked at the rust spots on his car and struggled to peel away the new layer from a roll of plastic wrap, just as I did.

As the weeks went on, I noticed that several people always walked to the front of the church to wave at the Poor

Clares; every once in a while, I'd even see a small flurry of hands waving back. I also noticed that before Father Senan offered communion to the churchgoers, he went first to the Poor Clares' grated sanctuary and gave them communion, his hand dipping in and out of an open window into their hidden space. I started to sit on the side of the church where I could look directly into their enclosure; however, it was crosshatched by the carved wood, and I had a hard time making out their faces. At the end of every mass, I watched them file out of the enclosure. One sister always stayed behind to roll down a screen over the open fretwork, thereby closing themselves off from the world again.

Since my Christmas Day visit to the church, I had received a few cards from St. Paul thanking me for donations to this or that fund. One was an invitation to a Valentine's Day luncheon for donors to the St. Paul Restoration Fund, and I decided to go. After mass, I followed others to a large second-floor room. The room was full of tables, each lavished with flower-filled centerpieces and candies, each place setting embellished with a four-inch plastic nun. At the back of the room was a banquet table loaded with kielbasa and sauerkraut and other hot dishes; at the front, just under the outstretched arms of a soft-eyed Virgin, were dozens of gift baskets stuffed with candies and fruits and little cheeses. I hoped one of these wasn't intended for me and began to feel guilty before I even sat down. I had only donated ten dollars to the fund. If I walked out with a basket, I would feel overcompensated.

The people sitting at my table were pleased to hear that I had started attending church after an absence of more than thirty years. "You're making the Lord very happy!" said a woman with an enormously shaggy fur coat. I could see that many of these people were not part of the regular group I saw every Sunday, and I later learned from Father Senan that they were longtime donors to St. Paul Shrine. Some had driven in from Akron, Medina, and other nearby towns, and none was as humble in appearance as some of the Sunday regulars. The woman in the fur coat got into a long conversation with the man next to her about why the adolescent Jesus made his parents frantic by staying behind in the temple to debate theology without telling them—how could he show them so little respect? she kept asking. I followed this conversation with a sort of gleeful wonder and kept quiet. Did these people speculate about the behavior of biblical characters all the time, just as my friends and I rooted around the details of our contemporaries' lives? I couldn't imagine having this kind of interest in the Bible. Even the good Catholics of my youth were more interested in gossiping about other churchgoers than in speculating about Jesus and his—to me, at least—contrary ways.

After the lunch was cleared away, the gift baskets (yes, someone insisted that I take one) and centerpieces were all given away. Everyone stopped talking as a woman wearing exceptionally red lipstick rose from her table and strode to the front of the room. She announced that the Poor Clares were going to make an appearance, and a flutter went through the crowd; clearly, this was what everyone had been hoping for. After a few minutes, a heavy rounded door at the side of the room shuddered open; someone peered out and then pulled it closed again. As people began to line up near the door, I went to sit by Father Senan, whose table had emptied.

"Have you heard anything from the sisters yet?" I asked him. Six weeks had passed since I'd sent my letter to the Poor Clares.

He shook his head and flicked a few crumbs from his brown robes. "Go up and introduce yourself to them," he urged. "Let them connect the person to the letter."

So I did what he suggested and joined the line, though I had no idea what I would say to the sisters. The wooden door had swung open again, and now the people at the front of the line were talking excitedly, as if a group of rock stars had just arrived. I tried to peer around the people in front of me, but I couldn't see the sisters; I couldn't even tell whether they were saying anything to their visitors in return. As I finally got closer, I saw that they were standing behind a grate of delicately turned metal bars. There were about ten of them, all dressed in the same traditional brown-and-white habit as the plastic nun back at my place setting: the same white band circling their faces, the same brown veils, the same dark brown dresses gathered into sheavelike folds. They looked happy. They nodded and spoke softly.

But I lost my nerve. When the people in front of me finished speaking and I was propelled to the front of the line, I only said hello, ducking my face as if I were the cloistered woman who never got out in public. Then someone pointed out Mother Mary James, the superior, and pushed me gently in her direction. I had a quick impression of fine cheekbones and delicate skin and slender hands, a woman in her mid-sixties who would have been considered attractive in the outside world. "I'm the one who wrote the letter," I said, then glanced down, then looked up again. "I'm the one who wants to write about you." I didn't want her to mistake me for some of the ardent Catholics in the room, even though my letter had made that clear. Still, I worried that this church with its tiny band of congregants might be so eager for new members that they'd even snatch up a longtime scoffer like myself. And I didn't want to make a false promise, even inadvertently. I still considered myself less a believer than a sort of spiritual voyeur, watching other people go through the rituals of their faith from a safe distance. I had come far enough from my scoffing days to want *these* people to keep on believing in God, but I wasn't ready to cross that line myself.

She acknowledged my presence with a steady gray gaze and a polite nod, but seemed unconcerned about my request. "We've had so many things to do," she said, looking over my shoulder at the line of people jostling behind me. Her voice was soft, a silk scarf floating in the noisy room. "We haven't had time to think much about it yet."

I pondered Mother James's unfamiliar reticence later as I danced my plastic nun—she was playing a French horn, her veil lifted by the force of her song—across the top of my computer. Most people are thrilled to have someone write about them. A few refuse, knowing how often journalists botch their characterizations of people either through spite or just because it's so hard to get the details right. In either case, people tend to think it's a big deal. The impression I was getting from the Poor Clares, though, was that my proposal was so far on the periphery of their world that they could hardly see it.

After a few weeks, I thought it might help if I talked to

another Catholic sister, one whom I had met the previous year. Beatrice is on the other end of the sister spectrum: heavily involved in several social service organizations, she zips all over greater Cleveland to visit various programs and sit through countless meetings. Cheerily resplendent in a blazer and flowered skirt, she had told me before that today's sisters must be so connected to the world that they carry a Bible in one hand and a newspaper in the other. I wondered what she thought of the Poor Clares.

"Oh, they're very conservative," she said, her eyes widening after I told her the reason for my visit. "I don't think they'd be very comfortable talking about themselves—about their ministry, maybe, but never about themselves." Then she went on to tell me much that I hadn't known about St. Paul. I had assumed all this time that people kept coming to the church because they were drawn to its marble angels and painted ceilings, or maybe to the kindly and charismatic Father Senan. But this was all wrong, Sister Beatrice said: they came for the Poor Clares, whose mission is to pray.

"They pray?" I said, my pen stopping in the middle of a line. "Well, *you* pray. All nuns pray. All sorts of people pray."

"They pray *all* the time," Sister Beatrice continued, her voice rising. "They pray all day and all night. They pray for the city and its people. They take requests from people who call in or write to them—they'll pray for this one's sick child or that one's aging parent. I think they even have a bulletin board outside their chapel, and they post the names there of the people who request prayers."

"They pray twenty-four hours a day?"

"That's their job"—she nodded—"and that's why people are devoted to the shrine. They want to make sure the Poor Clares are able to keep on doing it."

"Would they even pray for someone like me?"

"Everyone," she said, regarding me with new interest.

Then Sister Beatrice told me that some sisters from a more contemporary order had visited the Poor Clares several years ago. One was concerned about the Poor Clares, who live in a big, windowless monastery at the back of the shrine. The visiting nun worried that they were hazardously isolated in a rough neighborhood and that their elderly members needed more comfortable quarters. She mentioned her concern to the Poor Clares' mother superior, who met them in a special room with a low wall and a metal grate, suggesting that the Poor Clares could move to a new complex where they'd be safe and well cared for.

"But they wouldn't do it!" Sister Beatrice said, as if still slightly dazzled by this. The Poor Clares' abbess told the other nun that they often climbed up on the roof of their monastery at night to look at the quiet city around them. There they prayed for the city, noting the twinkle of each distant light and the wavering lines of streets that radiated from downtown into the darkness beyond. "They wouldn't leave St. Paul, because they didn't want to leave the city," Sister Beatrice continued. "They were afraid they wouldn't be able to watch over it in the same way if they moved."

After this revelation, I went home and wrote another letter. This time I addressed it to Mother James. I told her how much more I'd learned about the Poor Clares and how I thought people would want to know that there was a group of women on East Fortieth and Euclid who were always praying for them, whether they were aware of it or not. I didn't expect to hear from them right away. I'd gotten the idea that their side of the enclosure was like another dimension in which time passed at a different rate than it does in mine.

Then I had a terrible depression for several weeks in which I couldn't seem to get anything done. It's hard to say what caused it: there were so many things wrong, although none was what you'd call cataclysmic. I was tired of having free-lance jobs fall through and even more tired that the ones that didn't rarely paid enough. There had been a leak from the upstairs toilet that dripped through the ceiling and ruined the walls and wallpaper downstairs. Two of my dearest friends were having marital troubles and another was having terrible health problems. My daughter was having a hard time at college, and my son never seemed to want to spend time with me. My husband's job had taken him away for weeks, and I was lonely. It was cold and bleak outside and would be for another few months. I wondered if believers managed to avoid these dreaded cycles of despair. If not, what good was belief?

There was nothing to do but wait. I continued to go to mass, observing the little dramas around me, gazing at the pictures on the ceiling, singing along with the hymns. Sometimes Father Senan's homilies annoyed me, but more often parts of them would stick in my head and speak to me for days. The St. Paul cast of characters continued to fascinate me: the black-browed lady, the man with the big head of hair, the woman with the cross and the sneakers, and, above all, the reclusive and still-silent Poor Clares.

On Ash Wednesday, I drove down for St. Paul's noontime mass in the name of research: I probably hadn't been to one of these services in thirty-five years and wanted to see what the crowds were like—if there still were crowds that came to these things. The answer to the last question was yes: unlike the poorly attended Sunday mass, this service was packed with downtown workers who did their Sundays in the suburbs but liked the nearby convenience of St. Paul for this annual observance. As I did so often, I spent a lot of time looking at everyone. There were more people at this service who looked as if I could know them, sit down with them, have an entertaining argument with them, even flirt with them if I weren't so relentlessly monogamous. At the end of the mass, they all began to line up so that Father Senan or one of the other priests could mark their foreheads with the ashes of burned palm. So many people stood for ashes that the center aisle was jammed with slow-shuffling bodies.

And all of a sudden I wanted to join them. Father Senan had said in his homily that the taking of ashes was for people who knew they were sinners and wanted to ask for God's grace. That could be me, I thought. Even if I doubted that my moral code was the same as that of the Catholic Church, even if my sins were mostly the small-minded, mean-spirited, loss-of-hope, faint-of-heart variety. I started to rise, then I sat down again. I put my coat on the pew, then hugged it to my chest. I stood to let the two women sitting next to me get out, then I sank to the pew one more time. I was afraid that Father Senan might not want to mark my forehead if I walked to the front of the church with the others, that he might lean down and whisper that you had to be a true believer to do this.

But when the true believers were nearly finished, I walked to the back of the line. I followed the gray and white terrazzo squares up the aisle, then watched as Father Senan mumbled his way along the row of people with their faces tilted up. I took the place of one who left and waited. He saw me and smiled; that in itself was a blessing. He pushed away the hair from my forehead and marked my skin with his blackened thumb, saying again, "Dust to dust, ashes to ashes." Then I was struck with feeling, and I nearly sobbed and had to bow my head to hide the tears. Back in my pew, I waited for the lights to dim and the people to leave. I watched another priest fold the book, snuff the candles and walk away, leaving only the one bright light shining down on the cross.

2

N o matter which way I moved, I was always facing the priest's back.

The mass had ended. Father Senan was standing in the doorway like a store greeter, his beard slightly green from the reflected sheen of his vestments. He was shaking hands and finding something to talk about with each of the few dozen people who had attended mass. I seemed to be the only one who couldn't get his attention. I was always standing behind the person who did have his attention, and just as soon as that person left and I stepped forward, someone else would pluck at his vestments and he'd whirl around again. I was left standing there to watch his brown friar's cowl swing through the air and bounce against his back, my question stuck in my mouth like an oversized pill.

Finally, he turned my way. "Kris!" His neat little silver beard lifted slightly as he smiled. "Are you going out to enjoy this beautiful spring day?"

It was a beautiful day. On my way to mass, I had seen two

huge guard dogs playing tag in a fenced parking lot down the street, leaping and yipping and pawing at the breeze as if they had been given the day off. "I will enjoy this spring day," I said, "but I wanted to ask you about the sisters first. Did they come to any decision about the book?"

"Yes." His tone was as light as ever, but one eye creased in disappointment. "They aren't interested. They don't want to do it."

"But, why?"

He shrugged. "I don't know if they think they have time for that sort of thing."

Not have time? It seemed to me that they had all the time in the world. How could you not have time if you didn't have children or husbands or meetings to attend? How could you not have time if your job was just down the hall and it didn't involve talking on the phone or actually producing something that someone else had to approve, embellish, or buy?

The idea of a book seemed dead; still, mass had become a bit of a routine and I liked it. I continued to enter the dark church week after week. Sometimes I remembered to take a bulletin and a hymnal; most of the time I forgot and sat there feeling stupid and wordless. I watched Father Senan and his server as they prepared for mass from behind the wooden panel to the right of the chancel, pulling their ritual garb over their clothes, then entered the church with a little tongue of hair flickering at the back of their heads. I watched people file to the front of the church for communion, wondering who would take the host in their hands and who would allow Father Senan to reach between their lips and drop it in their mouths, who would take the cup of wine held by one of the regulars and drink from it and who would pass it by. I watched how the regulars rose at different moments to assist with the mass. Sometimes they seemed to have their assignments mixed up; once the heavy-browed woman and a thin, pale, face-of-a-saint woman stood and moved toward the altar at the same time, then one of them made a serene hairpin turn in the center aisle and returned to her seat. I wondered if there were jealousies among the regulars, each eager to have a role in the mass. Or maybe it was the other way around: there were so few of them and so much to do to keep even the most basic rituals of the church going.

People started to make themselves known to me. There was a man who sat at the back of the church who always seemed to smell of stale marijuana; I liked to keep a two-pew distance. One day he swung around and held something out to me at the end of the mass: it was a holy card of St. Theresa, the Little Flower, a cloistered Carmelite nun who died about twenty-five years after this church was built. I tucked it into my purse and he nodded with what seemed like a secret, knowing smile.

Others of the regulars had started to give me a little wave after mass. One day Father Senan urged me to join them in the Guild Room for coffee and cake. The room had lots of dark wood around the windows and heavy sliding doors, with a doorbell next to them and a small sign saying "Ring for the sisters." I sat at one of the tables, near the man with the thick black hair. "I was telling her that we should ask you to sit with us," he said, gesturing at the woman sitting next to him. He introduced himself as Myron and told me he owned a bowling alley down the street.

"Do you come to this church often?" I asked him.

"I come to mass every day," he said, then laughed at the surprised look on my face. "That probably just means I'm the biggest sinner of all."

Myron introduced me to Lynn, a woman sitting next to him who looked as if she could have been the younger, more somber sister of Gina Lollobrigida or some other Italian actress from the 1970s. Then there was Madonna, a plain-clothed Carmelite nun, and Myron's niece, whose name I didn't catch. She was leaving Cleveland to join the air force, and while the rest of us talked, she was looking around the room fondly. After a while, she walked over to the sliding doors and rang the bell several times. It took several minutes, but finally the doors ground open and an elderly, hollow-cheeked nun leaning on a walker appeared. She stared at the girl intently, gripping the bars of her walker as if it might all of a sudden scurry away. Lynn leaned across Myron and beckoned me.

"That's Sister Mary Agnes," she whispered. "She's ninety-two years old, and she's been here for sixty-three years."

"I thought they couldn't come out and meet with people," I said.

"She's one of their externs. It's her job to deal with outsiders so that the rest of the sisters aren't distracted from their ministry."

It seemed to be a job that the elderly nun could barely manage. She continued to lean on her walker and stare in an uncomprehending way at the girl, who finally shouted, "I just wanted to say good-bye." Then the two of them disappeared behind the wooden doors.

As I kept going to mass, I wondered if all the words of faith floating around St. Paul might find a chink in my agnostic armor. I almost always liked Father Senan's homilies—it took me a while to figure out that this seemed to be the word for what I had called sermons—and often found myself scribbling notes in the church bulletins, eliciting curious stares from some of the regulars. Once, he exhorted people to become more involved with efforts against evil, to move away from our own tight, self-involved little lives. He referred to both the antiabortion movement and demonstrations in front of the U.S. Army's School of the Americas, the training ground for so many of Latin America's right-wing militarists. I grimaced at the first reference because I've always been pro-choice, applauded the second because I'd like to stand and shout outside the School of the Americas myself; I warmed to his overall message of compassion. "When someone asks you if you have a minute, tell them you have two," Father Senan said, lifting his silvered chin to send his voice around the quiet church. "Instead of looking at an unfortunate stranger and saying, 'There but for the grace of God go I,' tell yourself, 'There with the grace of God I will go.'" Other homilies were evocative but mysterious, given my ignorance of the Bible. Once he talked about Jesus—this time he said "Jaaaay-sus," sounding more Irish than usual—revealing himself to Peter on the mountain. Which mountain? I didn't know and hadn't remembered to pick up the bulletin that day. Father Senan kept talking about this mountain and how Jesus had Moses and Elijah by his side and that some kind of transfiguration took place. "You can take your troubles to the mountain," he said. "You can see God in the darkness. You have to focus on the subtle hints of resurrection." It seemed he was looking right at me, although I considered that he might be like one of those paintings whose eyes seem to follow everyone in the room. Still, these phrases became artifacts, layered with implication, which I would turn and examine for weeks.

Even though I sat through these services, I was still an outsider, an observer who scuttled outside after the mass and recorded my thoughts in my car. I resisted becoming part of the group in the Guild Room; I even resisted saying the prayers that I remembered from my past out loud because I didn't want anyone to think I was like them. It was true that the shrine beckoned to me, but I didn't understand why. I felt I wasn't what any of these people would consider a believer and I didn't want to pretend otherwise. I used to go to Alcoholics Anonymous meetings with my husband and feel the same way. I liked their homilies too and almost always heard something that touched me—someone's wrenching candor or a funny story from some droll and only slightly repentant rascal. Still, I wasn't and couldn't be a real part of those meetings because I wasn't an alcoholic; I fall asleep after one drink, vomit after two. When the group engaged in their mass incantation of the twelve steps, I kept silent because these words weren't true for me. I always felt that people were looking at me askance, sure that I was in denial.

By late May of 1999, I was still going to St. Paul but it had passed from being an intriguing dalliance to an obligation, onerous at times. Friends would ask me to a Sunday brunch or morning hike; damn it all, I'd think, I have to go to mass. I started to worry that unless I developed a deeper bond to St. Paul I'd drift away, just as I've drifted from so many things. I'm a dilettante by trade and by nature: I make a living as a general-interest freelance writer, springing from subject to subject, and my span of attention is intense but brief in the rest of my life, too. My husband loves to watch from a window as I work in the garden. I snatch up weeds for ten minutes, then get distracted by the dead leaves stuck in the middle of the rosebushes, then stop to move some stones, then stare at a dead branch in the oak tree when I throw my head back to get the hair out of my eyes. I get bored on a steady, smooth path, which is why I've never been able to stay at the same job for more than two years. I realized that sitting through mass week after week wasn't helping me understand what had drawn me to the shrine in the first place or what had made me cry on Ash Wednesday; I was just sliding around the surface of faith, and I was afraid that I would soon fall off. If only the sisters would talk to me, I thought: if only they'd tell me, one after another, how all their different paths wound up converging in this high place of faith. If only I could find a path of my own by learning about theirs— a path not to the inside of the cloister, but to some sort of life lived in faith. One day as I was driving past the church, I stopped, backed up, and parked outside. I rang the bell at the church office and asked the receptionist if Father Senan was in. He came flying into the room wearing a T-shirt and shorts. I was dazed by his ordinariness.

"You're not a friar today!"

He had a bunch of papers in his hand and he glanced at

them briefly. "We don't always wear the robes," he said, amused, then shifted the papers to take my hand.

I looked around at the office, which was crowded with aging office equipment and had a fan balanced on every possible surface. "How about an article about St. Paul?" I asked. "Just a short piece in the newspaper's Sunday magazine? I wouldn't have to take up much of the sisters' time for an article."

"That might work," he said, rubbing his beard thoughtfully. "I'll ask them about it."

"I'll have to interview you, too. Once or twice."

"Me!" he said in mock horror. "Well, we can do that."

A week later, I was sitting with him in the living room of the friary, which is an old, converted nineteenth-century boardinghouse next to the front entrance of the Poor Clares' monastery. Entering this room was like walking into the 1970s: everything was brown, beige, and the color appliance makers used to call harvest gold. All the furniture seemed to be upholstered in earth-tone, for-all-eternity Naugahyde, in a pattern I now think of as Catholic tweed. I assumed all this had been donated to the shrine and had come out of someone's basement. I wondered if Father Senan groaned every time he saw another Barcalounger in this palette.

It was hot. I could hear fans whirring from other rooms in the friary, but they didn't cool me off much and I was in summer clothes; Father Senan was wearing his heavy brown robes. We sat in two tweed chairs with our backs to the street and a lamp between us. He kept his hands on his knees and I kept mine on my pad of paper and we rocked a little in our chairs.

"Well," he finally said, because I was taking too long to get started. "What can I tell you?"

"Let's start with the history of the church."

He told me that the diocese had published a book not long ago celebrating St. Paul's seventy-fifth anniversary as a Catholic shrine. "A bishop established the sisters here in Cleveland, because they wouldn't have had the money to do it themselves. Their vocation is to be prayers. To us, that would be a powerhouse."

"Do they still pray twenty-four hours a day?"

"Still." He nodded. "Now there are only sixteen of them, so it's quite a sacrifice. They have a secretary—there used to be enough extern sisters to handle administrative details like that—and of course they have an abbess. One of her most onerous jobs is taking care of outside distractions so that the others can concentrate on the Lord and contemplate him in prayer."

I made a face: here I was, a persistent wasp from the outside world, circling Mother James and distracting her from her ministry. Father Senan seemed to sense my discomfort. "She takes care of all the things in the house, too," he added. "The sisters come to her with requests for toothpaste, elastic stockings. . . ." He raised his hands and let them drop to imply all the other imponderables a group of cloistered nuns might need.

We talked for more than an hour. He told me he grew up in a Catholic household near Pittsburgh with a German father and an Irish mother, listened to religious stories on the radio as a boy, and linked the life of a priest with biblical dramas and grand adventures like the Crusades. When he first went to the seminary, his plan was to be a diocesan priest, meaning he would be attached to one diocese for the duration of his ordained life. But the seminary was run by the Capuchin order of Franciscans, a merry bunch who were free with jokes and song and lived in clusters wherever they did their work. All of a sudden, the life of a solitary parish priest seemed lonely and he decided to join the Capuchins. Fifty years later, he was living with four other friars who had various jobs around Cleveland, including one who ran a hunger center behind the shrine and one who worked in a nursing home. He himself was the pastor of two churches: St. Paul Shrine and Holy Trinity–St. Edward Church, which had a small, impoverished inner-city congregation comprising two dwindled, older congregations that were folded into each other some years ago.

I love to ask questions and tended to follow everything he said with a question. It meant that much of our conversation covered ground that was useless for the article, such as the intricacies of Catholic bureaucracy. "There are four orders of Franciscans," Father Senan explained. "Two browns and two blacks. Of course there are others but these are the main four, the ones that Rome considers true sons of Francis of Assisi."

"Which of the browns are you?"

"Capuchins, Order of Friars Minor," he replied promptly. "The other brown group, they have a nicer habit, much neater than ours. All of us have the three knots in our cords representing our vows. But we Capuchins have this long cowl. It's modeled after the European peasants' capuche, which they made by cutting the corner off a sack of grain and putting it over their heads when they worked outside. We show our solidarity with the poor by wearing this."

My hand was getting tired trying to keep up, and I had to keep checking my tape recorder to make sure it was working. "So you guys wear the cowl."

"Yes, the cowl, modeled after the capuche. Cappuccino the drink and capuchin the monkey both come from that root word."

He was sitting there placidly, his hands hardly ever moving from his knees, his lips clamped together neatly when he wasn't talking. I was starting to worry that this conversation was boring him, just as it was making me a little dizzy with arcana. I wasn't getting at the questions I really wanted to ask, either— like how one might detect the subtle hints of resurrection in the darkness. And I wasn't asking the questions that I needed to write my article, which had to be focused on the shrine's renovation project and not the connection between cappuccino and medieval headgear.

"You've never had any regrets about this life?" I asked.

He shook his head. "Not really."

"Is it kind of like falling in love, where you have all sorts of illusions at first and then come crashing down when reality sets in?"

He smiled. "Yes, I suppose it is like falling in love. It's never easy living with other people."

"Are you worried that belief is dying out? How do you feel when you walk into a church that was built for a thousand people and there are only twenty-eight scattered around?"

"I mentally count heads," he said, narrowing his eyes as if peering into the dimness at the back of the church. "I figure, 'That's thirty, that's fifty,' and my next thought is that I hope I have enough communion breads. I did that at a wedding on Saturday—I guessed about two hundred—but at a wedding you're somewhat safe because half the people aren't regular churchgoers and they won't come forth. We rarely run out anymore, although it used to happen all the time when I worked in the missions."

I wanted to ask more—more! more!—even though I was disappointed by his administrative, rather than emotional, response to this last question. I already knew that the ranks of religious orders are growing thin; the religious die or defect and then there aren't enough of them left to keep their ministry going. Father Senan had told me earlier in the interview that he had been a member of a central Ohio parish that lost its friars due to a manpower crunch. St. Paul had its hunger center because the Cleveland friary that had been running it closed for the same reasons. St. Paul itself might close someday if there aren't the people and funds to keep it going, and Father Senan's other congregation seemed to be teetering even more precariously at the edge of collapse. "What happens if the shrine runs out of people and money?" I finally asked.

"We turn out the lights and shut the door?" He looked down at his hands for a second. "It might happen."

I imagined the marble angels trucked away to some storeroom for retired icons, the frescoed flowers ruined by the leaking roof and crumbling from the ceiling, the Poor Clares themselves dispersed to a suburban church annex. It was as if Father Senan had confirmed the fatal diagnosis of someone I might have liked had I known them in time. "How terribly sad."

But Father Senan seemed to have a useful philosophy of detachment, saying that he would probably be gone before that day came. He explained that his life has worked on a cycle of biblical sevens—three seven-year stints at various missions in New Guinea, seven years in central Ohio, seven years in a couple of U.S. friaries, seven years at St. Paul by the millennium— and he was superstitious, unwilling to break the cycle. "Francis was a vagabond," he declared, "and that's the way friars prefer to live. It's a monk's job to stay in one place year after year."

When our time was finally over, I asked if he had heard from the sisters. He shook his head, then poked his finger at me. "Why don't you call them? I think that might work."

I quaked at this idea and put off calling them for as long as I could—for some reason, the thought of talking to them made me nervous. Still, I had convinced the *Sunday Magazine* editor to let me write the article and there was now a deadline to consider. One day I dialed their number, expecting whoever answered to tell me the sisters wouldn't come to the phone. Within minutes, though, Mother James was on the line. I could barely stammer out my request: Was it possible for me to interview one of the nuns for an article? What was I interested in? she asked. Everything, I told her. We set up an interview for that week, and she puzzled to find space on her calendar, making the little noises people do who feel themselves impossibly busy. As I started to say good-bye, she asked if I'd read a book about the

Poor Clares called *A Right to Be Merry.* "You should read it, Kris," she said with feeling. Her voice was light but urgent. "You'd love it. I just know you'd just love it."

Then something happened that seemed to threaten the entire project. Several days before my appointment with the nuns, I met with one of the parishioners. This was a woman who was helping Father Senan raise funds for the shrine's restoration and he told me she was a good source about its history. I had thought I was meeting her for an informal conversation but she was dressed for serious business and she had terms: I must allow her, the sisters, and Father Senan to review my article before I sent it to my editor. "I've worked with the media before," she said, fixing the kind of look on me that dog trainers use to make puppies sit and stay. "I know that this is possible."

"It isn't possible," I said. "I can read your quotes to you and I can go over the facts to make sure I've got them right, but I'm not allowed to let you read the article. No magazine allows that."

"Then there will be no interview," she said and turned her head toward the window, as if looking at the spot on the sidewalk where she expected to see me in just a few seconds, dragging my notebooks and minicassettes behind me.

"I don't understand your concern," I said, and I really didn't. "I'm not looking for scandal. I don't plan to be flippant about anyone's faith. I want to write about the shrine because I find it remarkable."

She nodded but wasn't mollified. "I know what the media can do," she said. "This place is precious to me. The sisters are like angels. I'm not going to expose them to anyone who might hurt them."

I gathered my things and stood in the doorway. "Well, they don't seem to share your concern since they're meeting with me in a few days." But as I walked down the sidewalk, I wondered if the Poor Clares would back off.

I was nervous as I headed back downtown for my scheduled interview two days later. I dressed with great care, wanting to look sober and respectable, but when I was almost there I realized that my black jumper and white blouse looked so nunnish they might suspect I was making fun of them. I pulled into the parking lot and felt immediately ashamed of my new car—all those vows of poverty so nearby, all those desolate-looking men who were sitting on the curb awaiting their free lunch at the hunger center. I parked under a tree so that my car wouldn't get too hot, then halfway to the monastery I realized I was stealing shade from the destitute. I stood on the sidewalk, shifted from one foot to another, looked at my watch, then ran to the front door of the convent.

I entered a quiet, cool alcove where a baby-faced man was dozing in a chair. When he opened his eyes, I told him that I was there to see the sisters and he smiled and pointed to another door. Mother James opened it before I even got a chance to knock. "Hello, Kris," she said in that quiet, urgent voice I remembered from the phone, and she turned and walked so briskly down a hall that I hardly had a chance to look around. She opened a door and motioned me into an odd little room that was divided in half by a three-foot-high white wall topped with a white metal grate that reached the ceiling. She called this room the blue parlor; I looked around and noticed that I was standing on a blue carpet. She left the room, and I sat in a chair positioned a few feet from the half wall. Then she and another nun entered the parlor from a door on the other side of the wall, and they sat in two chairs that faced me. Mother James pulled at a latch in the middle of the grate and folded its two middle sections to the side, like shutters. She introduced the other nun as Sister Thomas and the two of them looked at me through thick glasses that made their eyes seem dark and liquid. Their faces seemed untouched by time, white skin framed by whiter wimples, and their bodies were softened by the brown habits. Sister Thomas smiled all the time, Mother James not at all. I had a hard time speaking. I felt like someone who was courting them, looking up at the window into their world.

"What I'd like to know. There's a lot I'd like to know. . . ." I had a panicky feeling that I might babble like this for ten minutes. "I'd like to know what attracted you to this life that is so—extraordinary."

They looked at each other.

"Extraordinary in that it's out of the ordinary," I explained. "You know, a life that maybe only one in five million people would choose? Why did you?"

"It was the perpetual adoration," Mother James said in that silk-scarf voice. "It's Jesus, really Jesus, right there. We're going to be doing that for all eternity, adoring God. When you do this, it's like your heaven begins on earth."

"When did you know you wanted to do this?"

"I knew when I was six years old."

I was silent for a few seconds, remembering my old letters about angels. "I think that I wanted to be a nun when I was around six years old," I told her. "So what happened to me?"

I was rewarded with a laugh from Sister Thomas and a sudden, brilliant smile from Mother James.

They told me that they spent their days in prayer and work. They used to support themselves, at least in part, by making altar breads for the Greater Cleveland diocese. Several years ago, their ancient, creaky machinery broke down and they were unable to find replacement parts. Now they make their living as distributors, ordering the breads from outside the area and repackaging it for area churches. I asked if the churches came to pick up their supplies of bread, imagining a long dark line of priests standing outside their door on Saturday afternoons. Sister Thomas shook her head. "UPS."

They told me about some of the problems with the shrine. The roof was leaking, the plaster was falling, people came into the church and stole things, even the fans from the priests' confessional. Despite all this, they didn't consider their ownership of this building a burden; far from it. They were proud to be one of the few communities of religious women that had such a building; most have small chapels. Only the notorious Sister Angelica, who has made a small fortune at ecclesiastical venting on cable television and who used to be one of the sisters in the St. Paul monastery, has a building so beautiful. Besides, the monastery itself provided more than enough room for their needs. "A contemplative community needs a lot of room," Mother James said. "*Women* need a lot of room. When you live in a house full of women and you never get out, you need room."

She rolled her eyes and I imagined catfights in the hallways. "But someone just told me that you're all angels," I said. "Why would angels need so much room?"

"Angels!" Mother James said. "That's a good one."

They told me where they had come from and how long they had been here: Mother James had been with the community since 1964, Sister Thomas since 1959. Even after decades of living in the same space, they spoke with the accents of the places where they had grown up: Mother James with a flat Boston accent, Sister Thomas with the rounded vowels and well-hammered consonants of her Wisconsin heartland. When I pointed that out, they looked at each other as if they'd never noticed.

"Where are you from, Kris?" asked Sister Thomas, turning back to me as if just remembering her manners.

"California, but I live in Cleveland Heights now."

"I see." While she—or at least her robes—seemed to rise slightly when she asked the question, she settled back down again at my response.

I suspected that even though Cleveland Heights was only about four miles east of the monastery, she had no idea where it was—that she really had no idea where anything was anymore. Just to make sure, I asked.

"I'm afraid I don't," she said, a little embarrassed. "When you don't get out, you don't really know where these places are."

"Do you watch television or listen to the radio?" I asked, and they shook their heads. "Do you read the newspaper?"

"Oh, yes!" said Sister Thomas, clapping her hands. "We

get the Cleveland *Plain Dealer*—I just love that newspaper! We also read *U.S. News and World Report*."

All this time, I sensed a restlessness in Mother James. Then I recognized it: she was thinking about work. The two nuns had told me that the Poor Clares maintained a rigorous schedule of prayer. They met as a group five times a day to chant the Liturgy of the Hours, then carried on individually or in pairs throughout the rest of the day and night so that there was always someone praying in front of the Blessed Sacrament—the exposed host that they believed was the body of Jesus. Mother James must have a difficult job, I thought: there must be times when one of the nuns was sick or overslept or maybe even got scared in the dark church at night. She probably had to scramble to keep up this round-the-clock stream of voices to God.

"Why do you think people turn to you for prayer?" I asked Mother James. "Why do they call?"

"It's hard to pray when something terrible is happening," she said thoughtfully. "When a mother has a sick child, she has no time for it. But we do, all day and all night."

"Do people think your prayers have more power than their own?"

She shook her head. "I don't think so. There are just more of us and we do it together."

Throughout this interview, my questions were posed delicately, as if I thought these women were so frail that they might be crushed by the weight of a normal speaking voice. I even tried to keep my face blank, because many people say that

I unnerve them by staring too intensely during interviews. But I was becoming frustrated, longing for all the things I could not learn about them within this one hour. "How could you do it?" I finally asked. "I still don't understand how you chose this life."

They always looked at each other to decide which one would speak, and this time it was Sister Thomas who answered. I knew already that she had been an artist when she was a young woman. I knew that she still painted in one of the shrine's many extra rooms and that the smell of fresh oils wafts through the shrine on warm days. She told me that she had been raised Catholic but that it was art that had captured her heart. She had graduated from the Art Institute of Chicago, was rising in her field and had done a lot of traveling to work with other artists. She had even spent time in Mexico working with Siqueiros, the great muralist. She was at the height of that kind of life, getting ready for a major exhibit of her work, and she decided to take a short break in Rome. What could be better for a beautiful young woman? She had been thinking of doing more work connected with her faith, maybe trying her hand at stained glass; where better to see it? And then it happened.

"It was very sudden," she said softly, running her finger over the iron curlicues on the grate. "I was making pilgrimages to all the different churches during Holy Week and I was asking God to show me how to be closer to him. And he drew me toward adoration."

Right there in Rome, Sister Thomas made the decision that would carry her from her young life into this one in late middle age. She amazed herself and shocked her family because she had always been one to love all the great rambling possibilities of the world. Even the life of a sister in an active community had once seemed impossibly confining to her. "My personality began to change once I was drawn to the contemplative life," she said, looking from me to Mother James as if she was bemused by this transformation all over again. "I've never had any regrets. It was really the grace of God."

"It *is* the grace of God," Mother James said in an urgent voice. She added that someone once asked her why she hadn't chosen an active vocation. *Anyone* can pray, this person had told her. "That's not true," she continued, breaking into another sudden, brilliant smile. "It would drive some people crazy. It's a vocation, a calling to live our lives for prayer. It's God's grace."

I imagined a hand coming out of the sky to scoop them up and press them to the heavens. I shivered.

Writing the article didn't take long, but it was weeks before a date was set with the newspaper photographer. When I arrived at the church, the photographer was sitting in a red SUV reading my article. We walked to the friary and knocked at the door and Father Senan strode out in his long brown robes. He looked irritably at a can of pop sitting on the church steps, then noticed a workman nearby. "Is that yours?" he called out to him. When the workman nodded, Father Senan shrugged. "Well, that's okay. It won't ruin the picture."

A woman led the three of us to the Poor Clares' parlor. It was different from what I had remembered—smaller, cozier, and the white wall had a brown ledge at the top. "Before Vatican Two, there used to be a curtain there, not a grate," Father Senan whispered, patting the surface of the ledge. "That's how they had to visit with people, from behind a curtain."

The door on the other side of the room opened and Mother James, Sister Thomas, and two other nuns—Sister Maria and Sister Bernadette—entered the room. I introduced Dale, the photographer, and the nuns reached through the bars to shake hands. Dale asked them to move here and there, to tilt their heads this way and that, and they were very accommodating. They weren't at all shy. Their smiles were just like those of any women eager to preserve their radiance on film.

Then the four nuns left the room. Dale, Father Senan, and I walked into the hallway, and Mother James suddenly appeared in front of us, by herself. "You can come this way," she said and pushed at a door that opened into their private quarters. I had no idea that she was going to let us penetrate this far into their sanctuary. I hesitated for a second outside the door.

The inside of their monastery seemed much larger than its outside. There were five massive brick stories angled around a grassy courtyard at the bottom. The second floor had a wide, sunny balcony studded with stone pots containing a few dried husks of last summer's flowers. The third and fourth floors had covered balconies, and tendrils of vine waved from their pillars. This part of the cloister looked almost like an apartment building that had been folded in on itself, its outer edges tucked in neatly together. Everything was clean and quiet in their inner outside: the bricks looked as if they had been scrubbed, the courtyard statues looked as if they'd just been bathed, even the mop heads drying in the sun were a brilliant white. When I looked up, their own square of sky was a perfect blue. "This is it," Father Senan murmured as Mother James beckoned from the far side of the patio. "This is the extent of their world."

I was shocked that Mother James was allowed to share this unimpeded stretch of space with us—I didn't know that the rules of papal enclosure, which dictate the many ways in which the Poor Clares must separate themselves from the rest of the world, had a special loophole for newspaper photographers. Mother James gave us a quick history of the building—it had been built in 1930 for fifty nuns, with a special wing above the reception room for the new girls—then whisked us through another door. She walked close enough for me to feel her robe swish against my leg. It seemed shockingly intimate.

There were a few nuns already in the chapel who were genuinely praying and a few others who joined them for the photographer's sake. I hung back in the doorway while Dale went in, but I could see that the nuns' half of the chancel was far less grand than the one that faced the congregation. The back of the wooden panel that separated their chapel from the rest of the shrine was plainer on their side—in fact, the marvelous details that the churchgoers saw existed only in outline on the nuns' side. The back of their chapel curved along the rounded outer wall of the church and was ribbed into individual wooden cubicles containing a chair, kneeler, and prayer stand, one for each nun. The centerpiece of the room was the Blessed Sacrament, held in a great golden vessel called a monstrance. The monstrance sat in an opening in the wooden panel so that it could be seen from both the church and the nuns' hidden chapel. There, the consecrated host gleamed like a white eye within a golden corona.

Just as Mother James was starting to shoot restless glances at Father Senan, Dale finished his work in the chapel.

We heard laughter coming down the hallway; Dale and I inclined our heads that way and Mother James nodded. Two dark-skinned nuns were in the laundry room, shaking big white cloths between them and floating them over to a table to be ironed.

"These are Sister Claire Marie and Sister Aloysius," Mother James said, pointing to each of them. "They're our new members from India. We asked our monasteries there if they could send us some girls because we're down to so few here."

As Sister Aloysius wrestled with some mops leaning against the wall, Sister Claire Marie ironed an altar cloth, focusing her radiant smile on Dale even as he moved around the room to take pictures. Mother James stood outside the laundry room with one thin hand gripping the doorway, then burst into laughter. "Watch out, Claire! You'll burn your hand!"

It was decided that Dale would photograph Sister Claire Marie inside the church. "She's the most photogenic," Father Senan said. She put away the iron and ran down the hall, returning with a vase full of heavy red roses for the altar. Dale and the priest started to follow her down another hallway. I looked around to speak to Mother James and saw that she was already rustling off in the opposite direction.

"Thank you," I called after her.

She whirled around and put her hand over the pendant—it was a tiny golden monstrance with a gleaming miniature of the Blessed Sacrament—that hung from a chain around her neck. "When will the article come out, Kris?" she asked, her face pale in the shadowy hallway. "I'm so nervous!"

"I don't think there's anything to be nervous about," I

told her, suddenly stricken with apprehension. "I think you'll like it."

The article came out in mid-October, about a month later. I heard about it from all sorts of people, but I didn't hear anything from Father Senan or the sisters. I started to worry. What if they were offended by some phrase that had seemed perfectly benign to me? What if I had gotten all the facts wrong? What if I had only dreamed everything about the bishop buying the church from the Episcopalians, about the printers who attended mass in the middle of the night, about the cappuccino and the sacks of grain? I had to rummage through folders and consult my notes.

Then the phone rang. Mother James was breathless, confirming my earlier suspicion that time passes differently in their world. She sounded as if she had just read the article and hurried to the phone, while I had been stewing about it for a week.

"The article is wonderful, Kris," she said. "We've gotten so many calls. We want to get it reprinted in the Catholic papers. We keep calling *The Plain Dealer* for more copies because the girls want to send some to their families."

"See, you do have a story that people are interested in," I told her, seeing an opportunity. "I hope you'll rethink the idea of a book."

"What else is there to say? Besides, people have already written books about nuns."

"Not people like me." Meaning, not people who didn't know spit about faith.

She laughed. "Why would anyone want to know about us?"

"Not many people decide to spend their whole lives in prayer."

"It isn't our doing," she said. "The vocation is a gift, grace is a gift."

Then she started to talk about herself, surprising me with sudden volubility. She told me that her father hadn't been a Catholic and her mother was, but that he was the one who supported her decision to become a nun. When she was taking her final vows, a relative called and told her she should come home right away, that he was dying. She wasn't allowed to leave the monastery, so she asked God if he could help her with this problem. Her father had surgery and lived for another seventeen years. When both he and her mother were ailing in the late 1980s, she got permission from Rome to go home and take care of them. She missed the deep peacefulness of the monastery, but she stayed for six years, dressing in ordinary clothes, driving around town for groceries and other errands, and tending her parents until they died within four months of each other.

"There's so much sickness in the world," she concluded after a brief silence. "It's hard to know God's will."

"You must hear a lot of terrible stories."

"Our phone has been ringing constantly since the article came out! People calling with sick parents, sick children, sick husbands. When I get out of bed for chapel, there are so many people to pray for that I'm going from one to another all night long."

I was a little dismayed. I had imagined that the new calls were from people happy to discover this little group of prayers.

I hadn't imagined fresh cries of woe. I started to apologize, then realized that what I was hearing was gladness.

"There's such a great need for prayer," she said, her voice as still and bright as the air inside their courtyard. "Before your article, I don't think many people even knew we were here."

I didn't expect to hear from Mother James soon, but she called again a few days later to ask a favor. A company that designs Web sites contacted them with a special deal, and the Poor Clares had decided it was a good idea. They wanted to use my article for copy and Dale's photos, but the paperwork was confusing and none of them was very computer savvy. Could I help?

So a few days later, Mother James and I were back in the parlor. We sat on either side of the wall with the paperwork scattered between us. Each of us had our elbows on the ledge and looked through photographs.

"How long ago was this taken?" I asked, pointing to an old picture of her. Even with her hair covered and her severe garments, she was a nice-looking woman.

She smiled as she looked at the picture. "That was twenty years ago. I was forty-five."

I knew that by that time, she had already been abbess for five years. "It's a nice picture."

"Nicer than that one in *The Plain Dealer*!" she exclaimed. "I look like Morticia the undertaker's wife. Not that I care for myself and it's all for God's glory, but who's going to want to join us if we look sad?"

Our pile of pictures seemed pretty meager, but Mother

James told me we couldn't use a lot: the company would charge extra if they had to scan more than six pictures. She told me how much they had agreed to pay for the Web site and it seemed like a lot.

"How did they find you?" I asked in alarm. "Who are they?"

"We've already signed a contract," Mother James said, waving away my concern. "We have to go through with it now. If we don't get enough hits in a year—isn't that what you call them?—then we don't have to do it again."

I felt fiercely and suddenly protective. I wondered if the Poor Clares might have fallen victim to some kind of scam— after all, they probably wouldn't have the time or the savvy to do comparison shopping. How many ways might skilled commercial predators be able to fleece them, especially after reading my article about their otherworldly life? I had started thinking that the Poor Clares were like one of those tribes that explorers discover in remote jungles, living in perfect harmony with their land and gods, but I knew that such stories often ended with disaster: ruinous publicity and exploiters often followed the explorers. I wondered if the guardian at the gate—the parishioner who wanted to turn me away when I was writing my article—had been right. Would I be the one to ruin the Poor Clares' splendid secrecy?

*H*ow is it that I don't know spit about faith? Did you wonder about my saying that in the last chapter? Did you wonder how someone who went to Catholic school for six years could be so ignorant about Catholicism? I'm also clueless about Christianity in general: I've only read the Bible in connection with college literature classes, and I'm much more familiar with the Old Testament because it's been reinforced by so many hours watching movies like *The Ten Commandments*. When I went to Catholic school, we never read the Bible—that seemed to be something Protestants did, although this seems to have changed—and whatever I had to memorize from the Catholic catechism I've long since forgotten. When the Poor Clares and others at St. Paul Shrine seem perplexed that I know so little about the different saints and religious orders and rituals and prayers, I blame it on California. I tell them they practice Catholicism *Lite* out there. Midwesterners tend to think that's a sensible explanation.

But it's not completely true. There were children at St.

Thomas whose family life was steeped in the church. There were families who seemed to have a child in every grade and who had priests over for dinner and who managed to produce a priest or nun themselves once or twice a generation. My family was not like that. I was the only one of my parents' five children to attend Catholic school, and it was only because my mother had lost confidence in Oroville's public schools by the time I was born, eight years after my closest sibling. My brothers and sisters had a more distant relationship with the church, partly because in the early years of the family's life they lived in places where there were no Catholic churches. Here's a favorite Ohlson story. My parents had finally moved to a town after living for years at the edge of remote logging camps, where my father worked his way up from timekeeper to manager. One day my mother was out in the backyard hanging wet clothes on the line when my brother Dan burst through the back door, shrieking. She followed his pointing finger to the front of the house, where she found my sister Dorothy Jean, speechless and rigid with terror, flattened against the wall opposite the front door. A group of nuns were standing on the steps. They had heard that the nice Louis Ohlson who just joined their church had a passel of young children at home, and they were hoping to round up a few of them to begin lessons for their First Holy Communion. My siblings thought the nuns were monsters with cloaks and mummy bandages around their necks.

The only dedicated Catholic in the family back in those days was my father, and he was a quiet man: he never talked about faith and you'd never know how deeply religious he was unless you observed his weekly routine or knew how generous he was to dozens of charities. He grew up among Swedish farmers in Nebraska; his Italian mother was a naturally chatty woman, but all that Swedish reticence must have muffled even her after a while. He had a grandmother who had saved her egg money for years to return to Sweden but never told anyone of her plans: she just disappeared one day. None of the family remarked upon it when she left, and they soldiered on without her. When she returned a year later, neither she nor they commented on her absence. That's how silent they were. The longest discussion my father and I have ever had about faith went something like this. Me: "Have you *always* believed in God?" Him: "Well, sure."

Even though my parents were married in a Catholic church, my mother never went to mass herself. For years I thought she was just too busy on Sunday mornings; she always waved my father and me out the door, saying, "I've got other things to do." Over the years I discovered that she was actually skittish around Catholics, despite the fact that she had married one. She grew up in the midst of a big, boisterous Irish family—not her immediate family, but that of her mother, Dorothy—that had dumped the church years before she was born, their collective revenge on a mean and domineering Catholic grandmother. I doubt if the Catholics pined to get the Crosbys back; certainly, there was much about the family to discomfit the church, even around Reno, which is where they all lived. One great-uncle's business dealings alone would have been a major sticking point. According to family stories, he owned the land on which an infamous brothel ranch was located and, by accounts other than my mother's, had lively congress with the madames and prostitutes there when he went out to collect the rent. My great-uncle also boasted of other dubious dealings: he'd convince members of a local Indian tribe to catch wild horses for a case of whiskey, then sell the horses at a huge profit.

The church would have also looked with thin-lipped disapproval upon my grandmother. Dorothy was a handsome redhead whose parents had urged her to marry a prosperous older Catholic named John Bolte. He had a good job with the railroad and his family had a general store out in Nebraska, but it was a terrible match: Dorothy shocked the people in Fremont with her unladylike, Reno-spawned behavior, and she taunted my grandfather about his stiff Germanic ways. They fought and he was violent; my mother tells me that he once knocked her out cold, then commanded his two little girls to help him carry her upstairs and inform callers that she had a sick headache. Dorothy divorced John in 1920 and took my mother and aunt back to Reno, managing to work in two other failed marriages before she died at the age of forty-eight. Her siblings welcomed her back, but John's cruelty confirmed everything they already believed about Catholics. My mother now says she can almost forgive her father's behavior: he was sick and he drank and he was miserable. She can't forgive the hypocrisy of the other Catholic men living nearby. They gossiped about Dorothy, but waited until John left the house so that they could chase her around her kitchen. They even chased her when she kept her two little girls at home by her side, erroneously thinking that the men would have to muster some kind of propriety around the children.

Even though I can't recall it, my mother must have overcome her aversion to church when I was baptized. Most Catholics are baptized at birth, but my parents waited until I was seven, right around the time that I had my tonsils out and bit the doctor who was trying to put me under with an ethersoaked cloth. I know I wasn't taken to mass when I was a baby, as so many children are: I was old enough to walk and talk and be a skeptic. My father and siblings and I walked outside after my first mass and someone asked how I liked it. "Too much advertising," I said, a remark that made the Oroville paper. At some point my father began to take me regularly, but mine was still not the kind of Catholic upbringing that many of my Cleveland friends had in which they collected holy cards and all the girls were named Mary and the parish was the social hub. The only sign of Christianity in my house was a wooden cross that hung over my parents' bed. When they were occupied in some other part of the house, I'd stand on their pillows and take it down to examine it. The top part slid off to expose a hidden chamber with two white candles and a bottle of something— holy water? oil?—and I would play with these things until I heard a noise in the hall and shove them quickly back into the chamber. Once I broke one of the candles, but no one ever noticed. When my parents moved to a new house after I finished fifth grade and all my brothers and sisters were gone to college and beyond, the cross disappeared. So did the painting that my father had persuaded my mother to sit for, which hung on the other wall of their bedroom. She was glamorous in that painting, with a deeply plunging neckline and more rouge than she ever wore—and no freckles. She hated it.

When I wandered into St. Paul Shrine that Christmas Day, I wasn't connecting with the church of my past: I had stumbled onto a church from someone else's past. St. Paul was majestic, breathtaking, massive, more like a church in Rome than the one I had known in Oroville. Moreover, it suggested that whole fever pitch of religious activity that I had never experienced as a child, only on a far grander scale. As I was soon to find out, St. Paul had been the epicenter of a particular kind of Catholic fervor: people from all over the city came for something they could find nowhere else. Even though there were mostly only the echoes and bones of that St. Paul left, I was fascinated by them. It was useful to tell people I wanted to write a book about it: whether or not it ever got published, I was able to ask questions and sniff through old papers and thoroughly indulge my fascination.

I learned that the church that is now St. Paul Shrine represents the third attempt by area Episcopalians to maintain a congregation among Cleveland's monied elite. Their first building was on East Fourth and Euclid, now a bleak downtown commercial area of bargain shoe stores, a shop selling roasted nuts, and a shuttered department store. However, this church—a wooden structure—was never used. A young man set it on fire the day before it was supposed to open so that he and his friends could rush in, snuff the blaze, and emerge as heroes, but they bungled the job and the fire roared out of their control. Cleveland had yet to establish a paid fire department, but six volunteer fire-fighting groups raced to the church. Each was hoping to claim the quick-response reward that the city had offered to any group that was the first to arrive at the scene of a fire, but three of the companies pulled up to St. Paul at the same time. They immediately began to argue about which of them had arrived first and brawled as the church burned to the ground. With donations from across the city, a brick church was built upon the same site. Within a generation, however, the congregation outgrew this space. In 1875, the third and most magnificent St. Paul was built some thirty-five blocks farther to the east in a wealthy garden district known the world over as Millionaire's Row.

I learned most of this in a short drive to the shrine, merely by having Tim Barrett in the passenger seat of my car. The Cleveland Restoration Society had told me that Barrett was the man in the know about Cleveland's historic churches and I had already heard of his Sacred Landmarks tours, in which he ushers crowds through Cleveland's remarkable old churches and answers just about any question put to him—who carved the statues at St. Stephen's, what technique was used to make the stained-glass windows at St. Josaphat, which church was the first in Cleveland to have a permit for electrical wiring, and so on. I finally got Barrett on the phone to ask him what he knew about St. Paul's history. He offered me a private tour, so I went to pick him up in front of Cleveland City Hall, where he works as an architectural design consultant. When I arrived, I saw a wiry, purposeful-looking man staring into traffic from the main steps, and I coasted through a traffic light and pulled over. Barrett jogged to the car and almost reached it before the Cleveland policewoman who handed me a ticket with silent malevolence. I couldn't sputter for too long about the ticket, though, because Barrett was starting to rattle the papers in his lap. "I think I've brought most of my notes," he said.

As we drove to the shrine, Barrett peered at the city with unrestrained enthusiasm. I was reminded of the way it is when I walk my dogs, how every bush and tree and rock has a hidden olfactory significance of which I am completely unaware. Barrett seemed to know about each building we passed, what was there before it, and what was there before that. I was still fuming about the ticket and don't recall much of what he told me except that the tiny curbside shrine next to St. Josaphat—he suggested I make a side trip there—was constructed of fitted aluminum sheets instead of the stone or cement more commonly used. "I call it 'Our Lady of the Diner,'" he said with a giant grin. "Isn't it wonderful?"

By this time, I'd already gotten to know a handful of worshipers who were drawn to St. Paul Shrine. I guessed that they came for a variety of reasons: some because of the Poor Clares, some because of the Franciscans, some because it was within walking distance of wherever they lived, some because they could hide themselves in the shrine's big, shadowed, empty spaces and put their faces in their hands and carry on a whispered conversation with God without drawing much attention. I talked briefly with a few of these people after mass, but for the most part I kept a courteous distance. I didn't want them to get the idea that I was about to join them—as a long-retired member of a group of Vietnam War–era radicals, I knew how eager small groups are for converts. Still, I liked the idea of getting to know the Poor Clares through the people who had an attachment to them. I figured I could get to know the parishioners later, when I had a clearer sense of whether I could ever share the passion that drew them to the shrine.

Barrett had a different kind of passion. He had told me over the phone that of the dozens of historic churches left in Cleveland, St. Paul Shrine was one of his favorites. "It's one of the finest examples of sacred Victoriana in the city," he had said. "We aren't creatures of the cave, we're creatures of civilization, and that's what these historic churches represent." Barrett's interest was literary as well as aesthetic: he loved these churches for the story they told about the people who built them and lived during their heyday. For him, the shrine was both a magnificent structure and a document of the Victorians' quirks. For me, the shrine was the mysterious retreat of these women who still continued to feed the fire called prayer. I wanted Barrett to help me imagine its heyday and think about whether people would ever flock to that fire in such numbers again.

When we arrived, the Poor Clares were chanting the Liturgy of the Hours, an ancient Christian practice in which special prayers are said at five designated times of day. I couldn't tell if they were chanting in English or Latin: it was the kind of praying that sometimes sounded like song stuck on a single note, sometimes sounded like the register the human voice hits just before tears. Only a few worshipers were in the pews, and they barely glanced our way. One had blotches across his forehead and was weeping with abandon. This was the first time I had ever been in the shrine when the Poor Clares were gathered without a mass under way, and I was struck by the strength of their hidden presence. Their chanting resonated inside my head, just behind my eyes, and I was tempted to slip into a pew to listen. But Barrett continued walking toward the altar. He stopped near the first pew and flipped a few pages of his notebook.

"These grates look like they're made of wood, don't they?" he asked in a whisper with great carrying power, pointing to the panels that surrounded the chancel. I hurried to catch up. The grates created separation for the nuns, allowing them to worship the Blessed Sacrament in their chapel behind the altar and to observe the mass from their room at the left of the chancel. The space on the right was for the priest to pull the vestments over his workaday monk attire. The grates were impressive from the back of the church and even more so up close, with a row of stern, sharp-winged angels along the top and a layer of wine-colored glass obscuring any openings in the chiseled curlicues.

"Oak?" I ventured.

Barrett shook his head, pleased that I had made this obvious but erroneous choice. "They're actually plaster. Even though they were constructed in the twentieth century when the Catholics took over the church, they have the spirit of the nineteenth century. The Victorians were far more interested in fantasy than fact, and they would have enjoyed the faux look." He bent down to examine the grates on the priests' side, tapped at a pinhole, and made a small noise of affirmation as plaster dust drifted to the floor.

As we tiptoed down the aisle on the left of the church, Barrett discoursed on the many details that showed how much wealth was poured into the church's construction. While it was built right after a major depression, he said, there was no skimping on architectural luxuries and the final, elegant details didn't accrue over a period of ten to twenty years, as they did at many churches started during the 1870s. Barrett pointed at the elegant stone tracery around the stained-glass windows and the massive pipes from the church's original organ, which had been one of the largest in the city; these were evidence of money lavished on St. Paul. He rapped on one of the central pillars, and even though there wasn't a corresponding gong, he said that he had heard they were metal encased in plaster—unlike the timber-in-plaster pillars in most contemporary churches—the metal being a gift from some manufacturing baron. He pointed to the magnificent show far above our heads, the soaring Gothic Revival truss work with scalloped edges and overlays of wood that create a quatrefoil, a design echoed in other parts of the church. He exclaimed over the lushly painted corbels that hold the trusses to the wall.

"The Victorians were fascinated with color and pattern and texture." Barrett paused to admire the painted flowers that twine around the wall over the altar. "For them less was not more. They couldn't imagine why anyone would leave a wall blank. We call it 'horror vacui'—fear of a vacuum."

Barrett exhausted his notes on the main part of the church, and we went to the upstairs room where the Valentine's Day luncheon had been held. The Catholics called it the Lady Chapel, named after the hundreds of chapels in Europe dedicated to Jesus' mother, Mary. They used it for meetings and lesser events. At one end was an altar with an elaborately spired and gilded canopy—there, Barrett explained, to highlight the presence of the Blessed Sacrament in the monstrance below, much the way an extravagant hat calls attention to its owner's face. The altar itself was a hollow box, with a glass-paneled enclosure just under its marble top. Inside, a life-sized plaster saint reclined on a bed of plaster roses. Barrett knelt down and tapped the glass.

"That's probably a reliquary," he explained. "In Europe, churches have entire bodies of saints under their altars. Since there aren't enough saints to go around in the United States, churches here have pieces of them, like bone or hair. They bury the pieces inside plaster statues."

"So there's a real piece of that woman inside the statue?" I asked. The idea both repelled and excited me: it was so primitive, so weird, so magical in an eye-of-newt kind of way.

"I think so," he said briskly, then got up to pace the room. He sniffed the air, as if he were assessing a stew that was burbling in some far-off kitchen. "I guess Sister Thomas hasn't been working today. Her studio is back there"—he gestured at the wall behind the altar—"and sometimes when I take tours through here we can smell her oil paints."

Barrett walked the room pointing out other features, then leaned back to stare at a window shaped like a quatrefoil in the tiny triangle of wall just under the highest peak of the roof. Even from the Lady Chapel, we couldn't make out the design on the window—you'd have to be a bird or someone on a tall ladder to see it clearly. "How like the Victorians to go to all the time and expense to put in a window that's almost hidden!" Barrett exclaimed as if he'd just discovered this oddity. "It wouldn't make any sense to us to put a window way up there, but to the Victorians that hole makes sense." I tipped my head back to gaze at the little window, sure that the Victorians would approve of the scalloped mirror I had hung above the clock in my living room. It was only a few feet from the ceiling, so high that the only thing it reflected was the hickory tree hanging over my neighbor's garage.

On our way out, we stopped to return the key to the Lady Chapel to Marian, one of the lay women hired to answer the Poor Clares' phone and door and help them in other ways. "Is that really a reliquary upstairs?" I asked as she slipped the key back in her pocket.

She nodded and smiled at me, pulling a sweater the color of the Lady's blue mantle against her very black skin. We'd already spoken on the phone a few times, and she was happy that an outsider was taking an interest in the sisters.

"Whose relic is it?"

She slapped my arm with playful remonstrance. "St. Theresa!" she said, adjusting her glasses as if to get a better fix on my ignorance. "The Little Flower!"

Outside, Barrett sighed. He waved his hands at the parking lot across the street, the social services center on one corner, and the manufacturing headquarters on the other, as if trying to erase them. He wanted me to imagine the neighborhood as it was when the Episcopalians built their church there. John D. Rockefeller had already made a fortune selling grain, meat, and produce and had gotten his start in the oil business ten years before the church opened; his main house was on the opposite corner from the church and his summer home some five miles east of it. Across the street was the mansion of Jeptha

Wade, a financier, promoter of the telegraph, and resident eccentric. He was a spiritualist who was afraid that church bells might frighten his spirits, and he made the Episcopalians an offer: he would arrange to have the massive bell from their old church moved and installed at the new St. Paul as long as the church agreed never to ring it during his lifetime. Up and down the street were the mansions and gardens and fountains and arching elm trees of other prominent families—the local aristocracy born of railroads, shipping and iron ore, and banking—and St. Paul was the city's premier site for society weddings and funerals.

But by the year the Catholic diocese bought St. Paul in 1930, this world had already spun off its axis and rolled to the east. The Episcopalians built a new St. Paul church in Cleveland Heights, not far from where I live. The Rockefeller, Wade, and other mansions were still standing near the old church, but the wealthy families were long gone, lured away by the seductive mobility of the automobile and new enclaves for the very rich like Shaker Heights.

Commercial development had also encroached upon the former Millionaire's Row, and the Catholics used this trend to argue down the price of the property. In a letter to the Episcopalians, P. S. Mahon, Bishop Schrembs's representative, argued that the Episcopalians had overvalued the church's land, "which is the only real marketable value this property has." Mahon went on to say that a massive commercial project on Public Square that was completed in 1928 and resulted in Cleveland's signature Terminal Tower building (now updated with a new Hard Rock Cafe!) had "greatly depreciated the value on Euclid Avenue and that further financing and plans for an almost unlimited development by these people has retarded the progress and development of Euclid Ave for many years to come." Mahon offered $250,000 for the building. The Episcopalians countered with a "firm" $308,000. A month later, Bishop Schrembs made out a check for $5,000, a deposit on a final price of $257,000.

I tracked the drama of this transaction in the archives of the Cleveland Catholic Diocese. Barrett had told me everything he knew about St. Paul Shrine; my next step, he said, was to visit Chris Krosel, the diocesan archivist, who knew everything about the history of Cleveland's Catholics. The day I went to see her, I had botched the time and arrived at her office before she did. By the look of her dark windblown hair and sturdy black shoes, it appeared she had just stepped out of the wind tunnel that is one of Cleveland's major downtown streets. I offered to wait until she was ready for me, but she told me to come in. I stood in the doorway for a minute, staring at the collection of obviously old and sacred objects that were hanging on her walls and leaning against her filing cabinets. Then I noticed she was sitting in her chair, still in her coat, waiting for me to get down to business.

"What exactly do you want to know?" she asked in a tone that didn't sound exactly welcoming.

"I might be writing a book about the Poor Clares over at St. Paul Shrine, and at least part of it will look at the history of the church itself." She had already asked me this question over the phone, and I had scribbled a response in the car in an attempt to appear more focused than I had in that earlier conversation. Part of the problem was that I didn't want to narrow my search: I wanted to forage through diocesan records for interesting tidbits. I also just wanted to sit there and let her talk. I knew she was another mighty cloud of knowledge like Tim Barrett. I'm always happy to be drenched by such people.

"I believe there was a history written about St. Paul," she said.

I nodded. "I want to be able to set St. Paul's current situation in the context of the overall decline in inner-city churches, and Tim Barrett suggested you could help me do that. I'm also curious what happens when these churches close—how is this decided and what happens to all the religious objects that were inside them?" I glanced at the clothed and crowned statue of Jesus in a glass dome on top of her bookcase. As she followed my gaze, I hoped I hadn't given her reason to suspect I was an antique dealer on a scouting mission.

"The Catholic Church is a hierarchy and all decisions about church closings are worked out with the bishop," she said in a careful voice. "You'd have to talk to the diocesan lawyers about the disposition of property. I don't have anything to do with that."

"I heard there's a big warehouse where the diocese keeps all the old statues and windows and things. And then I guess they're recycled into new churches?"

"That happens sometimes, yes." Krosel pushed at the corner of her glasses and continued to look at me warily. "It's very important that you tell me exactly what you want to know."

I tried again but achieved no greater clarity. She sighed,

blinked her heavy-lidded eyes a few times, and started to talk about the increase in life expectancy among European peasants in the nineteenth century and how this resulted in fathers having too many sons among whom to divide their land and how this trend kicked off immigration to the United States and how many of the immigrants were attracted to Cleveland because its steel mills and salt mines and machine shops needed muscle and not necessarily muscle that spoke English and how the growing immigrant communities each wanted a church of their own. Actually, this was only a strand, a highly concentrated strand, of what she talked about for the next one and a half hours. It was an amazing mass of information that started funnel-shaped with the history of just about everything and worked its way toward St. Paul Shrine. I realized that Krosel's earlier blinks were like the flickers on my computer screen when I launch a Yahoo! search. Her questions about focus weren't evasive, only necessary, because she knows so much about so many things that she could talk for days. I sat in a chair and took notes, stopping occasionally out of sheer, dumbstruck admiration. She'd talk and talk, pausing now and then to smile indulgently at me, then begin a new strand.

The immigrants pooled their assets to buy adjoining parcels of land and ethnic communities took root, she explained. Many were built near the industries where the first wave of immigrants had found jobs, and each built its own church. It wasn't even unusual for there to be two Catholic churches nearly side by side, where the different neighborhoods met. When new waves of immigrants arrived in Cleveland, they often got off the train, looked at the skyline, and followed the spires of the church that was in their own ethnic style to find the right neighborhood.

The early immigrants became more prosperous, and their communities edged farther away from the sooty blast furnaces and foundries where many continued to make a living. As newer waves of immigrants took over the neighborhoods, they took the neighborhood church and converted it to a Catholicism with their own national flavor: thus the French-Irish Annunciation Church on West Twenty-second became the Hungarian St. Emeric. Other pressures forced even greater change. While the first- and second-generation immigrants lived comfortably within their ethnic communities and institutions, the third generation started to chafe under the burdens of ethnic identity. After the Second World War, this eagerness to shed ethnic identity fused with the new American love of the suburb. Affluent families had already been moving away from the city, but now even working-class families scrambled to leave. The romance of the picket-fence life was heavily promoted in the media, according to Krosel. "If you were a parent, the message was that you were almost a slacker if you didn't move your children out to the suburbs," she said, ending this line of thought with another, more rueful smile.

As people streamed from the city, urban churches and parochial schools began to struggle with dwindling congregations and resources. Krosel traced the decline and eventual demolition of St. Agnes, a beautiful cathedral-style church on Euclid Avenue. St. Agnes was at the far end of the same Millionaire's Row where St. Paul was built, and like St. Paul, it was more the embodiment of class than ethnicity. By the 1940s, St. Agnes's neighborhood had changed and the mansions had been carved into apartments or razed for commercial development. Urban blight set in as the new building owners let the properties decline. "They had no covenant with the community, no pride of place that led them to maintain the properties," Krosel said, then took a deep breath for the rest of this sad story.

The white population around St. Agnes fled to the suburbs and the black families who took their place had few Catholics among them. Krosel offered the statistics without even having to look: only 1.52 percent of Cleveland's African Americans were Catholic at the time, compared with a mere 3 percent nationally. Still, the pastor at the church made a valiant effort to attract a new congregation and began a series of outreach programs. Then came the death knell, Krosel said: the city began to neglect services in the area, effectively leaving the people and the church to flounder in ever-increasing blight. By the 1970s, the church needed $1 million in repairs and had a congregation of fewer than one hundred people. The diocese and the congregation finally decided to close St. Agnes, making it the first Cleveland Catholic church to fold because of dwindling numbers. Before the building came down, the diocese tried to track down the original families who had donated stained-glass windows and other religious art. The rest were auctioned off. Years later, Tim Barrett and other church buffs discovered St. Agnes's beautifully carved confessionals turned into phone booths in area restaurants, its vigil lamps hanging over tables to light the path of fork and knife for diners. "That was the learning curve," Barrett had told me. "We learned that there could be a terrible misuse of these objects."

In that first meeting with Krosel, we never really talked much about St. Paul Shrine. Still, I seem to have passed some kind of test—maybe one of endurance—and she was quite willing to set up another appointment. I was just as willing to hear her talk for another two hours, but when I came back the following week, Krosel had piles of materials waiting for me: folders stuffed with papers, as well as diocesan yearbooks containing sixty-some years of records from every church in the area.

"I didn't know if you really wanted to go into the archive rooms yourself," Krosel said, sounding solicitous. "I don't know whether or not you suffer from claustrophobia, so I brought out whatever I could find."

I stifled a moan of disappointment: I was eager to go spelunking in the archives—just the word made my heart beat a little faster. But Krosel turned back to her desk and we settled into our respective work areas. The room and that whole wing of the diocesan offices were quiet. The phone rang now and then but Krosel addressed her callers in a low voice, and even the occasional priest who entered the room whispered when he saw me hunkered at the table. I had piles of yellowed papers to myself. Some were so old and fragile I couldn't believe I was allowed to touch them. A few were so private I felt I was going through someone's drawers.

The records were a hodgepodge of the tedious and the tantalizing. There were dozens of carbon-copy letters from the diocese about the appointments of various priests to St. Paul Shrine; with the exception of the names, they all read pretty much the same. There were the letters about the sale of the church to the Catholic diocese—beyond the transaction itself, the correspondence was only remarkable in that Mahon's letters contained a remarkable number of typos: in one, he signed his name after closing with "Tours very truly." There was a mysterious letter dated August 6, 1930, to Mother Agnes, the Poor Clares' first Cleveland abbess, containing only one line: "I am sending you a check for $500 which you will understand." It was simply signed "Chancellor." There was also a series of dunning letters to Bishop Schrembs from the Daprato Statuary Company in Chicago, demanding payment for an altar it made at the bishop's request. The shrine's files reminded me of my own: stuck among the receipts from the roofers and the medical records and my children's report cards are things I'd be embarrassed to have anyone see.

In another file, old newspaper clippings showed that the Catholic diocese's purchase of St. Paul for a group of cloistered contemplatives was big news back in 1930. In a front-page article in the Cleveland *Plain Dealer*, Bishop Schrembs was given several column inches for a statement that seems, to the modern ear or at least to mine, odd in a grandiose sort of way.

"St. Paul was the most providential purchase I ever have made," the bishop wrote. "The church is to be given a new purpose that will make it to many generations as dear as the Basilica of Montmartre in Paris. It is to be a center of blessed activity on Cleveland's main thoroughfare, Euclid Avenue. Location of the Shrine at that point will permit adoration on a scale never before attempted in this part of the country." Does this sound strange because I don't think of adoration as something measurable?—scalable? Because I can't imagine today's Catholic Church buying even a small church for such an activity? Because my modern soul balks at the idea of adoration, a giving-over that seems to negate everything I've believed about self and will and ironic detachment?

Nine years before the diocese bought the church, the bishop had arranged for two Poor Clares from Austria to move to Cleveland. He settled them in a small residence east of the city, where they started the area's first adoration monastery, a chapel in which the Blessed Sacrament was visible and worshiped day and night. But the Poor Clares grew too numerous for that space, and the bishop was keen to move them and their "powerhouse of prayer," as he called them, into the heart of the city. He was jubilant after the purchase of St. Paul. The diocese retrofitted the church for its new role, ordering five new stained-glass windows from Europe that featured miraculous stories of the Blessed Sacrament, dividing the chancel in half with the mock-oak grates, and constructing a five-story, fortresslike monastery for the nuns adjoining the church, complete with an interior courtyard so that they could experience sunshine without breaking the rules of papal enclosure.

Father Senan had already told me that the shrine used to draw big crowds through the 1950s and even into the 1960s. Here in the materials Krosel had set out for me I found the historical records that gave statistical heft to this claim. I skimmed through the diocesan yearbooks. Leather bound, sweet smelling, the yearbooks allotted a page to each parish, handwritten in the gently looped Catholic penmanship I remembered learning back in first grade. St. Paul's first entry was in 1936. It boasted seven masses every Sunday and thirty-seven converts that opening year, more than any other church in the diocese.

More impressive still was a series of reports about the shrine that were written during the 1930s and 1940s. I learned that St. Paul was the flourishing center of the Society of Daily Communicants, a group that had been founded by the shrine's first priest and had members in the Philippines, India, China, Africa, and Europe. St. Paul itself had 1,051 members, people who came to mass every day for communion. There were also staggering numbers in other religious societies connected to the shrine: 465 people in the Nocturnal Adoration Society; 1,850 in Miraculous Medal; 2,045 in the Guard of Honor; and 11,640 in the People's Eucharistic League. These people were drawn to St. Paul because it was Cleveland's center for Eucharistic adoration; its devotees were a giant prayer circle that formed and re-formed throughout the days and nights. Who were all these people, I wondered, and why did the impulse toward this kind of prayer fade away?

One of the most curious documents Krosel put in my pile was a small gray pamphlet called "Sanctuary Chimes." It is written in the kind of cloying prose that I remember from certain children's books when I was a voracious eight-year-old reader who would zoom through every bit of text, even the stuff I thought was stupid. The pamphlet begins with a poem written in the voice of a plaintive Jesus: "I have not seen your face today, / Where were you? / A hundred others came to pray, / Where were you?" But however much the Jesus of the poem seems to be in a funk, the first chapter gives an impressive if florid account of the shrine when it was a place where thousands of people came to worship.

> *Just then a young lad, a truck driver, parked his White along the cross street and ran into the church through the side entrance. A moment later, he hastened back, whistling all the way, jumped into his truck and disappeared in the great traf-fic on Euclid. Presently two social workers and a district nurse entered; each carried a large brief case and an umbrella. Their tired step and exhausted appearance led me to think that they had been ministering to the poor and the suffering. They were followed by a crowd of week-end shoppers and a group of office girls.*

The writer goes on to catalog a continuing influx of railway workers, teachers, surgeons, florists, and athletes into St. Paul, all on one ordinary afternoon. The shrine seemed a virtual Noah's ark of the professions. "Who wrote this?" I asked Krosel. "Why is there no date?"

She inspected it and frowned. "Very elevated language. Obviously someone educated."

"It's a woman," I told her. "In the second chapter, people keep addressing her as 'dear Alice.' Why isn't her name on the pamphlet?"

Krosel looked as if she could discourse at length about this, too, but her phone rang. "Some people are embarrassed to speak publicly about their faith," she said, walking back to her desk.

There was nothing in the annual reports that spoke so eloquently as "Sanctuary Chimes" about the shrine as a beacon to the faithful. There was also nothing in the pamphlet that would prepare the reader for the present, when the shrine's doors are still open during the day but the visitors are few, when the cadre of hidden nuns has fallen from a high of fifty to only sixteen. I doubted that all the people who used to pray at the Shrine and their descendants were maintaining the old habits of adoration at other churches; it seemed more likely that in the process of assimilation their faith leached out of them along with their ethnicity. In any case, by the time my article ran in the *Sunday Magazine*, most people seemed unaware of the Poor Clares' existence. Some were amazed to find out that a monastery was just down the street from their favorite diner or just around the corner from the bank where they cash their paychecks. Others were jolted into the past by my article and called me to say so. "I was there as a child," they said, their voices dreamy and wistful. "I haven't thought about those wonderful nuns in years."

I was fooled by the friendly coffee-klatch ease of my meeting with Mother James to select photos for the Poor Clares' Web site. As it turned out, this moment of familiarity did not lead to others, and months passed before I actually met with her again. We spoke on the phone several times as 1999 drew to a close, but she was too busy to sit around answering my questions. The sisters were consumed with preparations for Christmas and the millennial New Year, and they had been hard at work with Kenny, the pianist, learning an elaborate vocal rendition of the mass. I could hear the evidence of their work during my Sunday visits to the church. Their voices had become stronger. One was particularly sweet: it soared and pulled the other voices in a radiant arc of song.

At some point, I realized I had gone to mass more times that year than in the previous thirty-five. I kept calling this churchgoing research, but it had become more than that. When I told yet another ex-Catholic friend that I couldn't do something with her one Sunday because I was going to church, she said, "Oh, you're so good"—meaning, I think, that she thought I was dutifully overcoming my true inclination to do something else. I told her that I wasn't being good: I *wanted* to go to church. It was amazing but true. Somehow, the act of going had created the desire to go.

However, the rest of my life remained much the same as ever; I might have been surrounded by holiness for an hour on Sunday, but it didn't transform the rest of my week. I did spend more time thinking about the implications of faith, though. If I started to believe in God, I wondered, would I then start to believe in angels? Miracles? Demonic possession? Would I be afraid to go down into the basement at night to pull something out of the clothes dryer, worried that unclean spirits might be seething and spitting in the dark cobwebbed corners? I remembered how confused my children had been years ago when they tried to sort out the pantheon of supernatural-seeming beings in stories: if there were no such things as fairies or unicorns, then surely, they reasoned, there couldn't be kings or astronauts or dinosaurs. In going to church every Sunday, I was obviously being drawn to something without consciously believing in it; it now seemed possible that belief itself might be closer than I had thought. So I had the inverse of my children's dilemma: If I came to believe that there was a divine presence, how far might I drift into otherworldly thinking? Sometimes I had to call my daughter at college and update her on church doings, just to hear the bracing echo of my own youthful scorn.

The year was scheduled to end quietly for JD and me. My daughter would be home for Christmas but then fly back to Oregon to spend New Year's Eve with her friends, my son had plans with his father, and JD's sons would be back in Florida. We tried to think of something madly festive for the New Year's countdown—something that involved my wearing a sequined evening gown and perhaps a tiara—but finally collapsed under the pressure of all that planning and decided to stay at home. We went to midnight mass on Christmas Eve at a church with a fancy congregation and saw one of our married friends there with his supposedly over-and-done-with extramarital fling. I went to Christmas mass at St. Paul the next morning and the nuns sang beautifully and the faces that were now becoming familiar smiled. Then five days later, my family had its own Y2K meltdown.

On the morning before the millennial New Year's Eve, I received an e-mail from my brother—written in the middle of the night—saying that our mother was sicker than he had ever seen her. She had come down with the upper-respiratory flu in early December that knocked off so many other eighty-five-year-olds and it had turned into pneumonia. For a week, she exhibited her usual confidence in her corn-fed Nebraska con-stitution and figured she would tough this out at home. Finally, her doctor put her into the hospital. She became well enough that he sent her home Christmas Day. She seemed to flourish for a few days, then stopped eating, became weak and dazed, and tumbled rapidly back into illness. When my other brother and his wife took her back to the hospital she weighed only eighty-six pounds—nearly fifty pounds less than I do and I'm much shorter.

I flew to California that afternoon and hunkered down near her hospital bed the next morning. I spent New Year's Eve there, watching celebrations break out around the world on a television that hung from the ceiling. I didn't know if she'd still be alive by the time this long-anticipated stroke of midnight hit California. She had dwindled even further over the course of the day and by the time darkness fell, she was too frail to turn over in bed or get up, too listless to eat or drink, too insensible or too hopeless to speak. When the nurses—a small brisk contingent of men who seemed to hail from all over the world—came to check her, they boomed and beamed and spoke as if this vacancy were normal. I kept telling them, "This is not who she is!" but they didn't seem to understand; maybe they thought I was just talking about the nausea or the weakness. Once when they were out of the room, she looked at me and whispered, "I'm not capable" over and over again. Once she whispered, "I'll be an object of pity." She stared at the wall with trembling lips, as if she saw a crack yawning to swallow her whole. Her eyes seemed like little more than blue pigment, even when I took her face in my hands and turned it so that we were nearly nose to nose. "Don't be afraid," I kept telling her, even though I myself was terribly afraid. "You're going to get well." Her hands are always cold but they were even colder then, clenched together in a rigor mortis grip above her chest. They shook violently, as if she were holding a bird in her hands that was struggling to break free.

I had told Mother James about my mother's illness before I left for the airport, and I asked her if the nuns would pray for us. Even though my belief in God was still more wistfulness than faith, I believed enough to want their prayers. While I sat next to my mother, I took comfort knowing that throughout the day and night this group of holy women held us in their thoughts. I imagined their prayers circling the two of us like soft, gray winged things. I could almost feel them brush the back of my neck. And maybe they gave me more than comfort: I felt strong at my mother's side, as if I had streaked across the sky on a rescue mission and was tugging her back from the brink of death. My mother finally fell asleep at 11:00. She woke up fifteen minutes later, sat up in bed, looked around the hospital room with shock and umbrage, and said, "How did I get back in this place?" And snap! she was herself again. She went home two days later. Within weeks, she was more robust than she'd been in ten years.

I stayed long enough in California to see that my mother was getting better and help my siblings set up a network of home-care nurses to monitor her and help my father manage. Even though the news kept getting better, I panicked every time I heard the phone ring after I was back in Cleveland. One of these calls—it was late January by then—was from Mother James. I had already sent her a letter to thank her for the Poor Clares' prayers, then followed up with a proposal to spend one day a week at the monastery getting to know the sisters. I had suggested that I could spend most of the day just helping out—getting their computer to work, answering their phones, or even mopping the floors—and then take two hours to interview some of them. But after Mother James asked for an update on my mother's health, she got down to the real business of her call.

"I can't do it, Kris," she said. "I can't let you in." I thought I heard regret in her voice, but there was no question about her tone of finality. I was sitting in my bedroom with the phone to my ear, watching the latest snowstorm—points of white against a gray day—cover the street as she continued. Having me inside the monastery would violate the laws of papal enclosure, she explained. Rome had recently been telling the Poor Clares to observe these laws more strictly than before.

"What about when I came in with the newspaper photographer?" I asked. "Why was it okay then?"

She made a quick, dismissive noise. "Sure, if we need a plumber or a painter or something that has to be done it's okay."

"How about if I come once a week and snake your drains?"

She laughed.

"All right, maybe not that. But I could come in and paint the hallway. It needs it."

"Kris, it's not about fooling Our Holy Father," she said, serious again. "The sisters wouldn't want you inside. And I don't even know if any of them are interested in talking to you. Thomas is the only one who seems to be excited about the idea."

I had a moment of panic. I didn't want to argue, but I also didn't want my window into the world of these remarkable women to be slammed shut. I quickly offered Mother James a revised plan. I suggested that I could still come to the shrine once a week, but I would go to the blue parlor for two hours and conduct my interviews there. Then, I suggested, I could spend the rest of the day helping Sister Regina, one of the sisters from India. She was the community's newest extern—a replacement for the elderly Sister Agnes—and was not bound

by the laws of enclosure. Sister Regina took care of many of the
community's outside chores. She also came out and joined the
tiny congregation in the Guild Room every Sunday after mass,
looking rapturous near the coffee urn, urging a piece of cake on
everyone, taking their hands as she talked to them. After one of
the parishioners had introduced me to her as the person who
wrote the newspaper article about the Poor Clares, she threw
her arms around me and declared, "God is working through
you!" in her melodically accented English. I had reported this
comment to my daughter, pointing out that this put me in the
same league as Joan of Arc. "Get a grip, Ma," she replied. But
aside from worrying that Sister Regina might view my presence
as some quirk of divine intervention, I liked her and would
enjoy spending more time with her. Mother James told me she
would put this proposition to the nuns at their next community
meeting.

While I waited for their answer, I was busy with so many
other things that I had to miss mass a few times. I went only
once, eager to pass another letter to Mother James giving further details of Plan B. Some things were still the same at mass:
Kenny gestured at the hidden nuns now and then as he played
the hymns, the man who always sat in the first pew by himself
turned and waved the congregation to their feet when communion started, and Father Senan ended the mass once again
with "Go forth to love and serve the Lord," bringing his hands
together and then flinging them out as if he were sowing seeds
in a marvelous garden. What was different now was the crowd:
it had easily doubled in size since my article was published.
Instead of having one of the fifty-foot pews to myself, I had to

share space. I noticed that lots of people were staring at the stained-glass windows and the painted ceiling and tilting their heads to get a good angle on the nuns' enclosure. These were the spiritual tourists, I figured.

On my way out, Lynn—the dark-haired woman who was always at mass, every day of the week—caught up with me. "See how many people are coming now?" she said, her eyes glowing. "And you ought to see it during the week. There are even more people then. We have one lady who's not even a Catholic coming every day since she read your article."

"Great." I looked at the people reading the "Canticle of the Sun"—St. Francis's lovely ode to the natural world—that hung on the back wall of the church. I wondered how long these new people would come to mass here, whether the shrine's bleak neighborhood was so far out of their orbit that this would be a singular visit. But I, too, had been a spiritual tourist. A year later, I had somehow become one of the regulars.

Lynn and I walked to the vestibule together, circling around Father Senan, who was surrounded by a cluster of people. All of a sudden, she stopped and peered at me. "Are you planning to convert?"

There I was, nailed in the hallway between two basins of holy water. "I have no idea," I said, and then I was curious. "Do I need to convert? I was raised a Catholic—I just haven't been one in thirty-five years."

"So you've been baptized?"

I nodded, and those glowing eyes grew even more intense. I wanted to change the subject—I didn't want to have this conversation in the middle of the hallway and wasn't sure I was ready to have it at all. "So where's your friend Myron, the guy who introduced me to you in the Guild Room last year? I haven't seen him in months."

A long alarming story followed. Myron had died about five months ago, Lynn told me. It was sudden and grievous since he had been her spiritual leader for the past fifteen years. When she first met Myron, she was a mess, she said—broke, sick, and troubled. Myron had told her that if she started going to mass every day her life would change, that God would guide her toward a better life. She did what he said. When she reported to him once that she had gone to get a physical and had a conversation with a radiology technician and found his job interesting, Myron laughed and asked her if God needed to be any more obvious: she should investigate this as a career. Now Lynn is a radiology technologist, healthy and without the other problems she didn't enumerate from years ago. She's still receiving the occasional heavenly signal, too: twice, she said, people she doesn't know have approached her with encouraging messages from Myron.

With that, I picked up the pace of our slow amble toward the Guild Room. This is the kind of story that spooked me about faith, just when I was starting to feel like it might have a place in my life—or that I might have a place within it. Weird little things happen in every life, and it's tempting to draw lines between them and then interpret these lines as a marked trail. Lots of people do this; whenever someone says "Everything happens for a reason," they're doing it. But this kind of reasoning always bothered me: if you celebrated the events that led to a good job as a series of milestones plotted by God, then it seems you must also blame God for the series of events that led to the genocide in Rwanda. But the people who praised God for the former rarely cursed him for the latter. And even if God arranged for Lynn to get a good job, why would he have employed such subtle clues to show his intentions? Why would God need to be so coy?

"How is your mother?" Sister Regina asked as soon as I entered the Guild Room. "We still pray for her every day."

"Well, you can stop now!" I said. "She's so healthy that my poor father can't keep up with her."

"Thank God!" Sister Regina's face was lit with jubilation. But I looked away, just as I had with Lynn. I felt that by engaging the look of triumph in Sister Regina's eyes, I would be agreeing that God had decided to cure my mother based on the nuns' prayers—and I couldn't do this. It was the same kind of hurdle that I couldn't clear with Lynn. Even though my awareness of the nuns' prayers gave me comfort when I was sitting with my mother on that miserable night, I didn't see why my mother merited divine intervention more than any of the other people who asked the Poor Clares for prayers. I couldn't imagine that *everyone* they prayed for had stories with happy endings. And why, I wondered, would God need to be asked to relieve someone's suffering? Couldn't he just figure it out for himself?

However, Sister Regina held on to my hands. "Why don't you go to communion?" she asked, and I had the sort of furtive, sort of pleased realization that some of the Poor Clares might be watching me during the mass, just as I watched them.

"I don't know what the rules are anymore. I don't even know if I'm allowed."

This was a dodge, and she seemed to know it. "What are you seeking at the shrine? Why did you come the first time?" She persisted and gave my hands a little shake.

The room was noisy and it was hard to follow what she was saying, as her English was sometimes hard for me to make out. "Loneliness? Emptiness?" I said. "It was some kind of longing. I'm not sure exactly why."

She folded my hands together and squeezed them. "How do you expect Jesus to come to you if you don't come to him? You have to tell Jesus, 'Fill me up. Take away my emptiness!'" She said this emphatically, as if she herself might get a little bossy in her dealings with God. Then she smiled broadly and turned away to help a few of the congregants find plastic spoons for their coffee. I left the shrine feeling blessed—by her, not God—and tried to do a good deed in the parking lot. A woman's car was stuck in the snow and Kenny the organist was trying to rock her out of the rut. I pushed at the front of the car, but I might as well have been pushing against the church itself. Finally, Kenny flagged down two homeless men from the hunger center. They sent the car skidding across the lot.

The day of the Poor Clares' community meeting came and went, but I didn't hear from Mother James. When she finally called, I had nearly given up hope. However, she told me that a number of the sisters were willing to talk to me—she named Sister Thomas and a few others that I didn't know—as long as they could read what I wrote before it was published. What about Sister Regina, I asked, but Mother James said she was much too shy for such things. We set up our appointment for the following Friday morning at nine.

By this time it was mid-February, a time of year that makes Clevelanders want to pack up and leave for good, and it was snowing heavily. I arrived at St. Paul ten minutes early in my effort not to be late. Knowing that Mother James had always been strictly punctual in our past dealings, I didn't want to disturb her so I passed the extra time walking around the outside of the monastery. The building seemed to have the power of anonymity: I had not only driven past it for years without noticing, but even now that I had been visiting the church for a little over a year I still couldn't have described the exterior of the monastery very well. As I walked, I ran my hand over the blocks of stone that were at the level of my shoulder. The gashes made by stonemasons so many years ago had been softened by the weather, and when I stood back and looked up, the effect was that of thousands of tiny sand dunes. The service entrance to the monastery was on East Fortieth Street, and on that side the wall held two huge bas reliefs of angels, carved into the same kind of stone. Still, the building was curiously opaque. Another world was inside, imperceptible to the city and its people.

I finally made my way back to the monastery's front door. Anne, a grandmother who works for the nuns part-time, opened the door, then dashed off to open up the church—it stays unlocked from 9:00 until late in the afternoon for anyone who wants to come in and pray in front of the Blessed Sacrament, which is on display at all hours except during the mass. She ushered me into the monastery's front room as she went, and Mother James and Sister Regina looked up from a table.

"Good heavens, Kris!" Mother James wasn't even in full religious dress: instead of the black veil that usually covers her head, she was wearing only the short white veil that lies underneath it and frames her hairline by a half inch. I felt like a guest who had arrived too early at a party, surprising the hostess in her bathrobe. "I never thought you'd make it out on a day like this."

"Her hair is full of snow!" Sister Regina cried, and ran from the room.

"I'm fine," I called after her, but she came back in with towels and patted my hair dry. Then Mother James sent me off to the parlor.

I had no idea whom I would interview this first morning. I also had no idea how long this arrangement would last. The door on the nuns' side of the parlor was slightly ajar, and I could see that it opened onto the interior corridor that circled their courtyard—in fact, I could see bare branches waving through the corridor's window. I remembered the day that Mother James whisked me and the newspaper photographer through the cloister, how stunned and almost disappointed I was that it was so easy to get inside. I wished now that I'd taken better notes, because it was probably the last time I'd ever see the heart of the monastery. I remembered standing in the patio, looking down on the trees and flowers and statues in the courtyard and up at the perfect square of sky. I had a feeling then that this was a holy place, that whether or not you were a believer it seemed high and hushed and rare, as if the very air shimmered from all those years of prayer.

Finally, Mother James herself came into the parlor. Two chairs were arranged in front of the low wall, and she pulled one of them back and sat down. She was still wearing the white veil, and the combination of the veil, the strands of silvery hair that just barely showed at the sides of her face, and her pale cheeks made her seem even more ethereal than usual. She looked at me wonderingly for a few seconds, then settled her hands in her lap. "I don't really know what I can tell you," she said a little apologetically.

But I had come with a plan. I had been reading about Clare, the thirteenth-century mystic for whom the Poor Clares were named. Clare had been a wealthy and beautiful noblewoman who became smitten by the preaching of Francis of Assisi. She arranged a secret meeting with him, at which he and his friars cut off her long golden hair and took her to a local convent. Then she moved into San Damiano, a church associated with Francis, and lived in poverty, prayer, and seclusion until her death. Other women joined her, including one of her sisters, and they were known as the Poor Ladies of Assisi.

It seemed that many of the leading religious women of that era were also wealthy and beautiful; what, I wondered, drove them to give up their lives of medieval privilege? What better place to start the interviews than with Clare, the founder of their order, the saint whose example had inspired these nuns to take this path? I imagined hearing stories about how they themselves had been smitten, one by one, by the beautiful Clare.

But Mother James only shrugged when I asked if she'd always been drawn to Clare. "Not really," she said, her Boston accent making her words sound more dismissive than they really were. "I always liked St. Theresa, the Little Flower. She was more for young people and her spirituality was so simple."

There were a few seconds of silence as I tried to think of another line of questioning, but I was stuck on Clare. "But don't you find her story fascinating?"

"Well, sure. She insisted that she wanted the privilege of poverty. She fought for it and asked the popes for it. They all said she couldn't live without money, meaning having a wealthy benefactor in the background to buy things for them." Mother James explained that St. Francis hadn't even wanted to have a monastery. He and his friars had what they called the Chapter of Mats. They slept outside at night on mats and wandered during the days asking for food. Francis initially had the idea that Clare would follow his lead, but the idea that women could live like this—unhoused and unfettered—was a scandalous notion at the time. Clare finally got her wish for poverty. She and her ladies slept on the floors of an unheated dormitory, and the friars brought them food. Clare herself fasted continuously on bread and water.

"Does anyone live like that now?" I asked about the bread and water and lack-of-heat part. "Wouldn't it be considered kind of odd?"

"I don't think you could live like that now." Mother James gave one of the wry chuckles that I was now used to, even though it was so at odds with her face and voice.

"Why would these wealthy women give everything up to live like that?" I couldn't imagine the young, rich, and beautiful of this country divesting their assets for a life of prayer. Still, Mother James and the other Poor Clares seemed happy—happier than the young, rich, and beautiful look most of the time.

"It's all the grace of God," she said. I slumped a little in my chair, since she'd offered me this explanation before and it settled no more for me now than ever. "You can't do it without his calling you and helping you see through that stuff."

Mother James's own struggle to become a nun had nothing to do with giving up the material world; for her, it was hard to leave the family she loved. She didn't enter the monastery at St. Paul Shrine until 1965, when she was nearly thirty, even though this had been the life she had been dreaming of since the age of six. During her twenties, she worked for an insurance company in Boston, went to mass twice daily, and spent her free time with her parents and a crowd of aunts, uncles, and cousins. "Oh, I was so happy with all of them," she recalled. "But I still knew I was going to be a nun someday." As she steeled herself for the inevitable time that she must leave her family, she realized that her dream might not come true, after all: she couldn't find an opening in any of the monasteries near Boston. Contemplative communities were built to be small, holding no more than fifty women, and they were all full. Some didn't even have the perpetual adoration that Mother James wanted—in fact, there were three other orders of Poor Clares with monasteries in Boston, but none practiced around-the-clock prayer. Her hopes rose when she found out about a Carmelite monastery that was under construction outside Boston, but when she called she found out that all the spaces were filled even though it would be years before it would open. Then she found out about the Cleveland monastery. After all those years of waiting, it was a little unnerving for the young woman when she came to Cleveland for a visit. She was interviewed by two eighty-year-old nuns in the room where we were sitting. Back then, the grille was constructed of dense, heavy bars and she could barely see them.

At that time, the Cleveland nuns were not Poor Clares, but part of another order called the Franciscan Sisters of the Most Blessed Sacrament. After Vatican II, this order changed its name to affiliate with the more well known Poor Clares, hoping to attract more young women, but it continued its original mission of perpetual adoration. "In a sense we were already Poor Clares because we followed the rule of the second order—for the enclosure—and we took the solemn vows," Mother James said, then she corrected herself. "We actually followed the mitigated rule of Pope Urban, not the rule of Clare."

I knew that the second order had something to do with St. Francis—his friars were his first order and I had heard someone speak of a third order for laity—but it seemed that if I asked one question about this I'd get tangled in the incredibly intricate web of Catholic orders, societies, hierarchies, and other mind-boggling distinctions. Mother James saw my hesitation and laughed. "This is all a mishmash to you, isn't it?"

Like the Poor Clares, the Cleveland nuns were governed by the strictest regulations for religious women. For the young Mother James, the toughest part was that they were confined to their chapel behind the altar. "We couldn't see the mass," she said wistfully, "and I loved the mass. We had to take our communion through a tiny door on the side of the altar. And we had to wear veils over our faces. That was so the priest couldn't see our beauty."

"So he couldn't see your beauty?" I repeated.

"Just kidding." She chuckled again. "At first, it was hard

for me not to see the mass because I loved it so much, but I got used to it. The hardest part—always the hardest part—was not seeing my family."

She stared past me for a few seconds. Her face was not animated even in conversation, and when she was silent she always looked slightly sad. I reminded myself that her decision to enter the Cleveland monastery had removed her from her beloved family for years: nearly four decades in a building six hundred miles from her home while her relatives died, dispersed, and grew into strangers. "Was it what you expected after all those years of waiting?"

She nodded without hesitation. "I had a library at home of about seventy-five books about religious life. I loved to read and I'd buy every book I could, especially about contemplatives. Of course, things are always different when you actually do them, but I was really happy here. I remember when a girl came to visit when I was a novice—"

Just then a bell rang somewhere in the monastery and echoed around the thick stone walls.

"What's that?" I asked.

"It's the bell for adoration. It reminds the sister who takes the next adoration hour that she has five minutes to get there."

We both listened. If anyone was rushing to make it on time, she did it quietly.

"And the girl who visited?" I reminded her, knowing that my own hour with Mother James was ending. "What about the girl who visited?"

"She asked if I was happy here. I told her that it was

beautiful, it was like being in heaven." Her voice was so quiet I might not have been able to hear it on the busy street outside the monastery.

After a few more minutes Mother James left and then Sister Thomas burst through the doorway. She rushed to the dividing wall and thrust her hands through the grate to take mine, then took the chair Mother James had pushed away and pulled it as close to the wall as she could and still manage to sit in it. I couldn't help but smile at the differences between the two women: while Mother James always seemed as if she'd just been tugged down from a higher plane, Sister Thomas was a bright bird of the physical world. It seemed to me that two women who have spent nearly forty years in the same small space would have taken on more of each other's personalities, more of each other's mannerisms and figures of speech. At the very least, I would think that their respective accents would have been subsumed into some uniform treatment of vowels and consonants. But this wasn't the case: Mother James's Boston accent was unmistakable, while Sister Thomas almost sounded as if she spoke English as a second language. Knowing her Wisconsin background, I always thought of a phrase from "America the Beautiful"—God's "fruited plain"—when she spoke.

Sister Thomas flung the grates aside and balanced a large black book on the dividing wall. It was a collection of photographs of the paintings she's completed in the monastery. With the exception of a painting of a soldier in Vietnam, which was commissioned by one of the shrine's benefactors, all the paintings were of biblical scenes. I thought they were quite wonderful, filled with movement and power and fierce emotion. The bodies seemed to have real heft, and they reminded me of the sturdy figures in a Diego Rivera painting. Sister Thomas was delighted when I told her this.

"He's the greatest artist of this century!" she said, falling back into her chair and rising up again. "That's a big compliment."

I studied the pictures and realized that I'd never seen a painting of Jesus by a woman. Just as all Michelangelo's women have—to my eyes—men's bodies, her Jesus had a more feminine body than any painting I'd ever seen of him. "That could be," she said when I pointed this out. "I wanted to show him the way he really was—as a man, yes, but he's also everybody."

"He's also very dark. You don't paint him as a pale European."

"Exactly!" Sister Thomas leaned over the wall to reexamine one of the photographs. "He was a Palestinian Jew. He had dark hair, dark skin, and he was outside in that hot Palestinian sun preaching. His skin would have been very dark!"

The Poor Clares' habits do a good job of muting physical characteristics. Their bodies disappear into a sheave of dark folds and their hair is tucked under veils. They each wear the same jewelry—simple gold bands betokening their marriage to Jesus, with his name inscribed on the inside, and a gold pendant of the Blessed Sacrament—and many wear thick glasses in *Father Knows Best*–type frames. I had to really concentrate to get a sense of what any of them looked like. As Sister Thomas went on talking about the inspiration for each of her paintings, I took note of her face: dark intense eyes, thick dark eyebrows, lips that were touched with pink, the way mine look when the lipstick has just about all worn off, but not quite. Her enthusiasm—for her vocation, for her paintings, for just about everything—made her seem young, although I knew she had entered the monastery in 1959, when I was only eight years old.

Sister Thomas told me that she had a number of projects going in her studio, and lots of new ideas for projects beyond that. She couldn't finish them as quickly as she'd like because her time was so limited: she was the community's treasurer and spent part of every day working on their finances, plus the demands of contemplative and community life kept her busy. Still, I was surprised at the number of hours painting that she said was "not much": six or seven hours each Saturday and Sunday.

After we finished looking at her paintings, I tried the same question about Clare of Assisi that I'd posed to Mother James. Sister Thomas nearly jumped from her chair.

"Oh, no!" she said with merry incredulity. "The thought of someone like Clare just went against me. I thought of this kind of life as a prison. I wasn't attracted to religious life at all."

"What were you attracted to?"

"Fun and good times! I went to the games and dances and swimming and bicycling and hikes. Later on, when I was older, I wanted to do something special for the Church, but when I was young I was all for fun."

In fact, her life as a young woman did sound like fun— and she certainly seemed to have more freedom than most girls in the 1940s. After she graduated from the Art Institute of Chicago, she went to Mexico and ran with a crowd of artists who had taken Diego Rivera and the other great muralists as their guides. All this time, her life swarmed with friends and dates—it was "a great life," she said—and then a romance ended badly. She went on to Italy, not long before a major show of her work was scheduled to open. She lived with an Italian family and traveled to Naples, Capri, and other sites. She visited many churches.

"I was saying a thirty-day prayer to our Lady because I really wanted to discern God's will for me." Sister Thomas stopped her discourse now and then as if to reconsider the mystery that was coming. "At first, I prayed to be very successful as an artist, but after a while my prayers began to change. What is God's will, that's what I started to pray for. At the Easter vigil service, I had a great grace from the Eucharist, and it was just overpowering. That's when my vocation started to take shape."

I could hardly wait until she finished to blurt my next question, which had been building steam the whole time she had been talking about her thirty days of prayer. Even though I hadn't arrived at any sort of intellectual justification for prayer, I had started doing it—furtively, skeptically, sporadically. Most of the time I was instantly bored or distracted. A few times the impulse stayed and I felt better, as if my cloak of petty concerns had slid away. Still, I couldn't understand how people made prayer part of their lives if it was dull most of the time, and I didn't know what they said or expected when they prayed, and I couldn't understand how they even remembered to do it with any regularity. I started asking around. One of my brothers told me that he prayed every time he walked outside to get the morning paper, that first breath of morning fresh in his face. A friend told me that she prayed when she walked from her car to her office. My Methodist-raised husband told me that he prayed every night before he went to sleep. I was intensely curious about this: there he was, inches away from me, and he didn't look like he was praying. For a few weeks I quizzed him about this after the lights went out. "Did you forget to pray tonight?" I'd whisper. "Or are you doing it now?"

I figured someone like Sister Thomas would have all the answers. "I don't understand prayer," I told her.

"Well, who does?" she answered quickly. "Prayer is a mystery."

She listed the many kinds of prayers that occupy the Poor Clares: vocal prayer when they say the Rosary or follow the Stations of the Cross; the Divine Office, which is chanted five times each day; the prayers at mass, and contemplative prayer. Of all these, she told me, contemplative prayer is the most mysterious of all.

"God leads us," she said. "We usually start with a meditation on something—maybe a reflection on scripture—but sometimes thinking is an impediment. Sometimes God draws you deeper, and sometimes he just wants you to remain in his presence and not reflect on anything."

She apologized for what she considered a poor explanation, saying that she was clumsy with words and that her insights were better expressed in her paintings. But I was intrigued by this sense of a presence that she was describing.

"You feel you're being led?"

"Yes, led," she said, as if excited that I came up with such a perfect word. "He leads and the reason it's so hard to describe is that he leads each soul in a different way."

"You always feel him there?"

She frowned slightly. "Sometimes there is the dark night of the spirit when it seems that prayer is impossible." Because of my readings, I wasn't surprised by the suggestion that hopelessness exists even within the Poor Clares' monastery. By the look on Sister Thomas's face, I guessed that it would be more painful there than anywhere. "We contemplatives have to live by faith," she continued, "and it's sometimes very hard. Sometimes we may not have any emotions or feelings or consolations in prayer, sometimes for a long period of time."

"Then how do you go on?"

She looked so solemn that I wondered if she herself had been through such a period recently. "He does not leave us without the strength to carry on in our religious life and in our prayers. We go on but it's difficult, and God permits this. It is a purification, so that our souls become more detached from our selves and we are freer to do his will."

"Many people have a dark night of the spirit all the time," I told her. "You haven't been out in the world for a long time. Most of my friends don't have any kind of faith."

Sister Thomas told me about her own crisis of faith after she went to Mexico: she was missing mass, arguing with other Catholics, and unable to stomach a lot of the church doctrines she now held as undisputed truths. "Maybe God allows you to have a crisis of faith because you can't just take your parents' or someone else's faith for your own," she said thoughtfully. "He wants you to find faith for yourself."

This was the closing note of my first day of interviews with the Poor Clares, and it was also the opening note of the following Friday's interviews. Sister Thomas came bursting through the parlor door again, pulled the chair up to the wall, and told me that Sister Anne Marie—who was interested in talking to me—had to have minor surgery and that Mother James had taken her to the hospital. Then she told me she had been thinking about our discussion from the previous week. "Everybody goes through a crisis of faith," she said. "The crisis helps us search our souls."

As she talked about how a crisis of faith leads to true faith, I kept my own thoughts to myself: that sometimes it does and sometimes it just leads to no faith at all. For most people, lack of faith doesn't cause a crisis because there aren't any external pressures to believe in anything but your own will and luck. You're more likely to have a crisis if you want to believe in God, if you start to believe, and this was the difficult path I was beginning to tread. I had invited my daughter to come to church during her spring break, thinking that even if religion itself had no appeal she might still enjoy St. Paul's art and architecture. I turned to find her glancing over her shoulder, grimacing as if she were in the middle of a scene from a very scary movie. "All these people sound like zombies," she whispered when the congregation was midway through the Our Father prayer. So I had to guard my growing enthusiasm for the Poor Clares, especially around my kids and many of my friends. If they thought what I was doing was journalism, that was all right; if they thought it was some kind of personal journey toward faith, that was a little alarming. The whole situation reminded me of a cartoon I had seen somewhere, probably in *The New Yorker*: a middle-aged couple looks out their living room window, and the man says something like, "It's the kids—quick, hide the cigarettes!" There was this odd role reversal going on: years ago, I was worried about my parents finding out that I had lost my faith and now I worried that my children would find out that I was looking for it. One of my best friends was on this same path toward belief, but had an even greater dilemma. She was Jewish and her parents were vigorously antireligious, having had a fight of epic proportions with a rabbi decades ago. Mara worried what her parents and her equally atheistic siblings and college-age children would say if they discovered that she was trying out different temples one by one: a few Orthodox ones, a few Conservatives, a Reform, and a Reconstructionist. "I'd rather tell them about my affair with Antonio!" she said, shuddering at the memory of a disastrous fling with a married man.

Sister Thomas mistook my long silence for confusion and apologized again for her clumsiness with words. "My gifts are not in long speeches or writing poems or anything like that," she said. "Well, I do perform in plays once in a while."

I perked up. "The community has plays?"

She nodded. "Either Sister Margaret Mary writes them, or sometimes we perform one of the plays that the sisters from India brought with them. Sometimes the plays are comical, sometimes they're spiritual. We do them for special occasions."

"Is there a need to break up the routine, since you're all enclosed here and with each other all the time?" I didn't want to use the word "bored," but it did seem that the sameness of the schedule and environment and people would get monotonous.

"It's not a problem," she said, probably guessing the secret, unspoken word, "but we're human beings—we like variety. There are other things we do for special occasions. Like right now, we're practicing hymns for a special Easter mass. And we have regular recreation."

"Like basketball in the courtyard?"

Sister Thomas had a way of treating everything I said seriously, even while she laughed. "Well, we used to play volleyball out there, but the ground is so uneven now that we're afraid someone will turn an ankle. We do have a bicycle that someone donated to us, but there's no place to ride except around the roof garden. To enjoy something like that, you really need to have grounds. Our Canton monastery and the one in Birmingham have grounds, so the sisters there could ride all over the place if they want."

I was thinking of all the fun Sister Thomas had in her youth. With her natural exuberance, I could easily imagine her pumping a bike down the sidewalk, even now that she's in her late sixties and is wrapped in yards of brown fabric. Again, she seemed to guess my thoughts. "I can't do that, but I'm happy here. We all seem to be happy here."

Sister Thomas went on to say that she has lived in great cities like New York and Chicago, and that she loved living in downtown Cleveland, loved the way the city's energy flowed around the monastery. She explained that she went up to the rooftop garden at night to watch the skyline; in the morning, she devoured the city newspaper and especially the arts section. She knew more about Cleveland's orchestra and ballet and community theaters and performing arts complexes, I thought, than 99 percent of the people who are actually able to attend shows at these venues.

"Everyone here seems to have their piece of the newspaper that they go to," she said. "Mine is the arts section. Sister Bernadette, she goes for the sports section."

"Everyone has different interests?"

"Different interests! Different talents, too. Mother James and Sister Mary Joseph, they have such a talent for organizing things. Sister Margaret Mary writes the plays. I couldn't write a play or a poem to save my soul."

I was still stuck on the image of the sixteen nuns gathered around the morning paper, each pulling away the part that linked them to the community of interests they left years before. I asked Sister Thomas if the nuns settled down again at night, the way my husband and I do, and talked about the front-page events. She nodded, then suddenly looked anguished as she mentioned a recent story of a young mother who had killed her two children. I could imagine her bent over the paper on the days such stories appeared, nearly unable to stand because of the pain. She seemed to feel things so keenly.

"These people need a lot of prayer." Sister Thomas sat very still.

I've always wondered if people with faith have an easier time dealing with stories like this. It seemed they must. If they were confident that an all-knowing God was holding life in balance, that these cruelties weren't stones that could pull the universe into a pit—if they had this confidence, if they had even a faint belief, it must make things easier. But Sister Thomas didn't look as though comfort were at hand. "I often think that if only these people who are killed could appear to us from heaven and tell us how God in his infinite wisdom permitted all this for a greater good—" She stopped, then smiled at me sadly. "You just wish sometimes that a miracle like that would happen."

Her hour was up, and she left. I didn't know who would be coming next or even, since Mother James was at the hospital with Sister Anne Marie, whether anyone would be coming at all. I listened for sounds in the corridor but could only hear voices near the monastery's front door: Anne, the woman who let me in every Friday morning, had brought her great-grandchildren to work and I could hear her low, calm voice answering their high, excited voices. I sat for another five minutes, musing over Sister Thomas's sad face, then started to gather up my things. But there was a sound on the other side of the wall. Sister Regina pushed the door open and stood in the doorway.

At first I thought she was just passing by and stopped to be polite. But after saying hello, she came into the room. She placed her hand on the back of the chair where Sister Thomas had been sitting, then slid into it herself.

"I didn't think you wanted to come!" I said. "I'm so glad you did."

She looked shy, but without any prompting began to tell her story. It was as if she had been standing outside the room composing herself and was determined to speak before she lost her nerve. She told me that she had been an extern sister in India for twenty years. When she first came to the Cleveland monastery three years ago, she was eager to give up the outside life and become one of the cloistered sisters in perpetual adoration.

"What was it like, that change?" I asked.

"It was so peaceful." She searched for words. "So prayerful. I thought that even if I was sent back to India, I would want to be on the inside forever. Then all of a sudden, something was telling me, 'Go out!'"

She started to become very animated, continuing the story as if she were carrying on an argument with someone near my right elbow. "I didn't know why this was coming to me—I *liked* being on the inside. I told Mother James about this. She told me Anne and Marian and the other laypeople are doing all the work on the outside—what would there be for me to do? I told her, 'I don't know, Mother, only this is calling me.'"

Sister Regina and Mother James decided that they would both pray about this. On the Feast of the Holy Rosary during morning prayer, Sister Regina received another strong message: Go out!

"I asked the Virgin, 'How can I explain this to Mother?'" Sister Regina extended her hand to the space near my elbow. "I don't know this culture. I don't know many people on the outside. Why is this coming to me?"

After morning prayer was over, Mother James walked right over to Sister Regina and the latter took this as a sign: usually, the two go in separate directions and don't speak at that time of day. They got into the elevator together and on the way to the next floor, Sister Regina talked of this newest message.

She told Mother James that she knew she wasn't a holy person who could perform miracles; still, something was telling her to leave the cloister. So the abbess told her to start making her way outside and see what God had planned for her.

Even after Sister Regina began to leave the cloister after daily mass and mix with people, it remained unclear what she was supposed to do with them. "I keep saying to Jesus, 'I was happy inside and now you're telling me to go out.'" Her voice quavered toward lamentation. "Then the answer finally came to me: I must start a holy hour for our people." She finally sat back in her chair and looked at me, although the answer still made trouble across her face.

Sister Regina knew a few people on the outside, and one of them turned up at mass the following Sunday. The nun told this friend that she wanted to start a weekly hour of prayer at the shrine, one that anyone could attend and participate in. The friend got a strange look on her face. She told Sister Regina that she had worked late the night before—she was a nurse—and had been planning to sleep in late, but that she woke up early in the morning with the feeling that she must go down to the shrine. So the two of them started to pray together for help in organizing a prayer hour. The friend called people she knew who might be interested. Another friend of Sister Regina's—an Indian engineer from out of town—called some "pious ladies" that he knew in Cleveland. Momentum was building. Still, after the prayer hour was announced in church, Sister Regina and her friend fretted that no one would come. Then Sister Regina received another message.

"One day I was so discouraged," she told me, her voice

full of urgency. "I'm a human being, and we sometimes doubt. Then I closed my eyes and saw a big man, very handsome, and some little soldiers following him. I felt the strength of God. I prayed and this mighty warrior turned and it's the face of Jesus. I understood then that he's in front of me. I said I'm sorry, Jesus, because I doubted you. And then I stopped worrying, because I knew that this was truly God's plan."

When the prayer hour finally convened, there were lots of people, around sixty. Now, she said, there were sometimes more, sometimes less. She was no longer discouraged.

I listened to all this, but had my usual doubts. Depending on who's reading this, my doubts will either make perfect sense or will be further evidence that I'm a bonehead. I didn't expect that Sister Regina was either delusional or making things up: she was the kind of person you instantly knew was both sound and sincere. But don't we all believe what we want to believe? Isn't that what the rash of false memories about satanic cults and sexual abuse proved a few years ago—that the mind can create a memory of something it imagines? Don't I walk around thinking that things I've dreamed really happened? Don't I still have the feeling that I'm one of Bruce Springsteen's intimates just because I had an intense summer-long fantasy about him twelve years ago? I found Sister Regina's faith and her words for it moving, but this was not the way I could be convinced. And I couldn't imagine what could convince me: even if I had a vision of Jesus, I would probably credit it to a stubborn fleck of LSD still bobbing around in my system after all these years.

I asked if her monastery in India was much different from the one in Cleveland.

"Very different," she said. "There, people come night and day to pray to the Blessed Sacrament."

"That's how this shrine used to be forty years ago," I told her. "Do you get discouraged that people don't come?"

"I know that people long to come," she said, opening her hands as if she were weighing the burden of their longing. "But if they can't, the sisters will pray for them. We have been given this privilege to be free from all kinds of things so that we can be mediators between God and the people."

Then she reached forward and put her hand on my wrist. "If you love a person, you can feel them," she said, her fingers rough against my skin. "I feel God. I relish him. I can taste what he is giving me. It's hard to find words for this."

I was thinking that her words were pretty impressive. Remembering Sister Thomas's catalog of talents in the community, I decided that here was the poet, this round-cheeked, black-eyed nun whose face was brighter than the overhead lamp.

"I'm so happy, but I would be even more happy if you could taste Jesus," she said, then sat back and shook her head. "I jabber a lot. I never get tired when I speak of God. When I was a little sister, I tried so hard to be good. But God doesn't need my goodness, he wanted my love. It's just like in your house. If you work and clean it and make it beautiful, what is the use if you don't spend time with your husband?"

She stopped talking for a minute, as if waiting for me to say something. But I had run out of things to say. I felt as if I were sitting in the sun.

"Look at me," she started again. "I'm ugly, but when I'm filled with God's goodness I feel more beautiful than anyone."

"You are beautiful." I thought all of them were beautiful—Mother James with her gray wondering eyes, Sister Thomas with her pink smiles, and this one with her shy radiance, but then I always think the people I like are beautiful. It pleases me to look at them.

"Yes, I am," she said, nodding her head serenely. "I am thinking of my good God."

Later that day, I ran into a friend whom I hadn't seen for about a year. She asked what I was doing these days, and I gave her these days' stock response: hanging with nuns. After I explained who these nuns were, she nearly dropped her armload of dry cleaning. "How wonderful!"

This was one of two reactions I usually got when I discussed the Poor Clares. The other was "How awful!" People seemed to be of two very different impressions when it came to cloistered contemplatives. Most men who weren't at least medium-core Catholics looked alarmed. They always asked about the sex: at first they looked disturbed, as if they couldn't countenance women who made do without the pleasures of men, then they perked right up again as they speculated about whether the nuns were pleasuring each other. I got so tired of hearing this question that it started to make me twitch. I had no problem understanding that you could give up sex if you believed God was calling you to a life that precluded it; people gave things up all the time for one sort of higher purpose or another. And I certainly knew a number of women who didn't have sex: they hadn't consciously picked celibacy, but they had chosen to leave bad marriages and hadn't found new lovers and were happy regardless. I was picking up the whiff of a double standard: the notion that celibate women were probably frustrated and neurotic and dried-up crones without the life force of semen pumped into them. On the other hand, there was the accompanying notion that monks and other celibate men were somehow ennobled by giving up their carnal desires—women, in other words. Or perhaps the people who found it so much easier to approve of male celibates just assumed that they were gay and that it was altogether a good thing to have their sexual activities bottled up by God.

This is not to say that all the women I talked with viewed the Poor Clares' choice in a benign way. Many looked horrified—the way, perhaps, that Sister Thomas used to look when someone mentioned this kind of life—as if these nuns had volunteered for genital mutilation. Many other women— feminists who approved of women living in community or soulful types who put great stock in prayer—thought the Poor Clares' monastery seemed an otherworldly delight.

By then I realized that neither of these perspectives was right. There was hardship in the monastery, but it seemed to me that it wasn't just the denial of HBO and cross-country skiing and new leather jackets that made the nuns' lives tough. Rather, the hardship came from their constant struggle for faith in a place where there was little to distract them from its absence. There was also joy, but not primarily from the time they spent in community or even in their escape from the strains of ordinary life. Their joy seemed to come from the times when their lifestyle held them closest to God.

I called the monastery the week after my interview with Sister Thomas to remind Mother James that I'd be coming again on Friday. Anne answered the phone and sighed when I gave her the message. "I don't know if they'll even want to do it this week," she said. "You know, Sister Anne Marie died."

I was incredulous. "But I was just there! I thought she went to the hospital for minor surgery."

"She died Saturday afternoon, honey. We buried her yesterday."

I was sure Mother James would be devastated. She worried terribly about the health of the older sisters—she had been living with most of them for thirty-five years—and the death of Sister Anne Marie must have seemed like the sundering loss of a parent. I also knew that she worried about the impact that the Poor Clares' declining numbers would have on their mission. She had once told me that some of their other monasteries had so few sisters that they couldn't manage twenty-four hours of prayer. She figured the Cleveland community could maintain the unbroken chain of adoration if their numbers stayed above twelve. With Sister Anne Marie gone, there were just fifteen nuns—and some of them were older and frailer than she had been.

I didn't get to console Mother James that coming Friday. Someone else was waiting for me in the parlor that week and the next, and I didn't want to disturb her with a phone call. The following Friday, the phone rang just before I was ready to race out the door. It was Mother James, telling me not to come: the flu was rampaging through the monastery and everyone was sick.

As always, I was momentarily stunned by her call. There was the gentle voice that I almost recognized when she said my name, and there was also the childlike thrill I had every time she said, "Kris, this is *Mother*." After I recovered, I told her how sorry I was about Sister Anne Marie.

"I didn't hear about her death until after the funeral," I said.

"It was very sudden." Her voice was even more hushed than usual. "We brought her home from the hospital and when we got up to the second floor, she just fell forward in her wheel-chair. She was gone by the time the medics got here."

"I'm so sorry," I said again. "I would have come to the funeral if I had known."

Mother James sounded thoughtful. "Yes, I wish you had come, Kris. You should have been here to share a death with us."

5

Sister Anne Marie's death shook me.

I had fallen into a comfortable pattern with my Friday-morning visits to the nuns. I'd tumble out my door at 8:45, speed down city streets where the dust was just settling after rush hour and the cops had left for their coffee break, and ring the monastery doorbell at 9:00. Anne would let me in, hurry off to unbolt the heavy church doors in time for the stray early worshiper, and I'd wander down the dim corridor to the blue parlor and wait for one of the Poor Clares to appear on the other side of the grates. It's amazing how quickly complacency sets in: after one month, I'd become almost flippant about this arrangement. I was reminded of *Tuesdays with Morrie* and started thinking of this as "Fridays with . . . well, someone." I couldn't come up with anything snappy.

But after Sister Anne Marie's death, I realized again how precarious this little community's existence was. Before her death, I had spent at least some of my time at mass trying to sort out the eyes, mouths, and noses behind the faux wooden grates.

I'd try to spot Mother James, Sister Thomas, Sister Regina, and then speculate about the others. There at the far right: Was that Sister Emmanuel? The one who took the chalice from the priest: Was that perhaps Sister Kevin? Was there someone new there, standing in the rows of dark shapes? It was almost like a game. But after Sister Anne Marie died, I was nervously counting noses, hoping each week to come up with the right number. If I saw a space where there was formerly a bowed figure, I'd start to worry that another sister had disappeared. I knew there weren't lots of other women rushing to take her place. Not that there was no interest in this vocation: Mother James had told me of a few recent inquiries. One was a widow with grown children, but the Poor Clares turned her away—they didn't accept anyone with children because they felt the longing to see them would be unbearable. Another woman was rejected because she had suffered a nervous breakdown years before. The nuns felt that their lifestyle was too intense for anyone with even a slight history of emotional instability. There had also been a more recent inquiry from a woman in Arizona, but no commitment as of yet.

When I went down to the monastery on the Friday after Sister Anne Marie's death, I wasn't sure if any of the nuns would come. I wasn't sure if any of them would ever come again. There were so few of them to begin with. Now that Sister Anne Marie was gone, the others probably had extra responsibilities; it was possible these meetings were an indulgence they just couldn't sustain. On the other hand, it was possible that Mother James might view these interviews with a new urgency, a way to tell the world about their way of life before the ones who had been living it for so many years disappeared. Maybe her heart lurched a little at the thought of my missed appointment with Sister Anne Marie. After all, she was one of the nuns who had wanted to talk to me.

And aside from its effect on my project, Sister Anne Marie's death saddened me. We had never met, but I had seen her that one time I went inside the monastery, trailing Mother James with the newspaper photographer. Sister Anne Marie had been in the nuns' private chapel when we arrived, a slight figure bowed down over one of the wooden kneelers in front of the Blessed Sacrament. She lifted her head for a second and smiled and what was a lined and slightly sorrowful-looking face suddenly became a sweet one. Then she bent her head again and that's the picture that was in the newspaper: a thin old woman in a black veil and robes, her forehead and glasses and the serpentine veins of her hand shining in the photographer's flash, a silent prayer caught between her lips. I looked at the picture after her death and wished I had been able to thank her for praying for my mother.

This Friday, I told myself not to take any of this for granted. I told myself to take in everything—even the details of the parlor.

So here's what it was like in there. Brass doorknobs in and out, warm to the touch. A dark wood table to my right, topped with a thick sheet of glass and a box of pale blue tissues. Five fake leather chairs, three brown, one yellow, one blue. On the wall over the table, a needlework angel accented with tiny gold beads; on the opposite wall, a framed picture of the bishop that looked pretty much like a college graduation picture from the 1950s, except that the robe and cap were different. On the nuns' side of the parlor, a matching table topped with plastic flowers in a basket and a statue of Jesus-as-shepherd. Two fake leather chairs, a folded bamboo screen leaning against the wall. Tan-painted walls on both sides with some mirror-image peeling, floors covered in blue flecked carpet. I had to look closely to notice these things: just as the nuns' garments muted their physical characteristics, the bland furnishings in the blue parlor muffled its distinctiveness as a place. The radiators thumped. Doors banged. I picked up the faint odor of soup.

Then the door on the other side of the grates opened and a brisk, sturdy nun walked in. "Hello, Kris," she said in a voice that made me sit a little straighter in my chair. She swung an arm through the grates to shake my hand, then settled herself in the chair with the calm authority of a CEO facing a meeting of compliant shareholders. "I'm Sister Maria."

At first I thought I hadn't met this nun before, but I quickly remembered that she was one of the four who posed in this room for the newspaper photographer. Yes, she told me affably, she was one of the four. Then I reached further back in my memory, to the day when I first saw the nuns face-to-face as they greeted people at the Valentine's Day luncheon. Sister Maria had stood to the left of the group behind the grated door. She had nodded and smiled, her cheeks bunching up into plump pink rosettes, but I didn't hear her speak. Something about her solidity reminded me of a woman I had seen when I was an exchange student in Austria and my host family took me on a trip to see little-known regional attractions. At one point, we crossed a river on a barge that had no identifiable motor, but when we reached the other side I saw that the barge was powered by a big-shouldered woman tugging a rope through a pulley. On the basis of this weird association and her silence, I conceived a notion of Sister Maria as Germanic, a non–English speaker. When someone at the luncheon said that the pastries were made by the nuns, I took this absurdity even further: I imagined Sister Maria rolling dough in the cloister kitchen, her habit steaming from the oven's heat, turning out the grupfen and other pastries that the women in my Austrian village made.

This was pure nonsense. Sister Maria not only spoke English, she spoke it fast and with street-smart regional gusto, as I discovered when I asked where she was from.

"Ha!" She chortled, looking very pleased, and proceeded to talk even faster. "As soon as I open my mouth people always ask me where I'm from. Can you guess?"

I shook my head.

"Philadelphia! Kensington, what's called the old northeast neighborhood. But I've been all over the place since then. I spent many years in the south, a year in New York, a year on an Indian reservation, and three years in Washington, DC, before I came here for ten years. I never seem to lose Philadelphia, though."

I remembered that Mother James had told me a little about Sister Maria back when we were talking about rich and famous women giving everything up to be nuns. She had explained that there were a few twentieth-century women who had followed in Clare's path. One of the most celebrated was Katharine Drexel, daughter of a Philadelphia banking magnate. After her father died, Drexel used the income she received from his estate to build schools and missions for black and Native Americans. Drexel wanted to become a contemplative, but her bishop persuaded her to start a missionary order to continue serving these communities. She founded the Sisters of the Blessed Sacrament in 1891, establishing the order's motherhouse outside Philadelphia. Over the course of her lifetime, she spent $20 million on behalf of black and Native American communities and founded New Orleans's Xavier University in 1915, the first such institution for African Americans. Since her death in 1955, two purported miracles involving inexplicable cures of hearing loss have been attributed to her and she was canonized in 2000. Sister Maria had been a member of Mother Katharine's order and had even tended her a few times when she was ill. This made Sister Maria the only Poor Clare in the Cleveland community to have been in the presence of a living saint. All the others made do with desiccated relics.

I asked Sister Maria when she knew she wanted to be a nun.

"From the first grade, if you can believe that." She planted an elbow on the arm of her chair and tipped her head onto her upturned hand. It was the kind of posture one might assume when smoking a cigar. "I went to a school where sisters taught. Our first-grade teacher would stand outside and watch us at recess, fingering her rosary the whole time. I looked at her then and said to myself, 'I want to be just like her.'" This image of the solitary watcher in rapt prayer didn't sound appealing to *me*. When I was in first grade, I would have probably stood in the shadow behind her and made faces.

Sister Maria tucked her decision to become a nun deep inside her, like a flower pressed in a book. But even though she didn't speak of it, people around her unwittingly steered her toward her vocation. When she was in sixth grade, one of her friends bragged about taking the streetcar all the way to the end of the city line. There, she said, was a shrine belonging to the Sisters of the Blessed Sacrament. Sister Maria was determined to see it and convinced her parents to let her ride the streetcar with her friend. After a few visits to the shrine, she was invited to a retreat. Later, one of the nuns approached her.

"She said, 'Mary Jane, *you'd* like to be a sister, wouldn't you?'" Sister Maria recalled, leaning forward and speaking in a confidential tone. "I had told myself that I wouldn't tell anyone, but I couldn't lie right after coming out of a retreat."

"Did you tell her?"

"I told her and she gave me the names of some sisters at the motherhouse. I went up there and I just loved it."

"What did you love about it?" Again, it was hard to imagine a little girl being so powerfully drawn to a house full of nuns.

"Their devotion to the Blessed Sacrament—that was the drawing card, even back then," she said, nodding her head vigorously. "It was exposed all day in their chapel. And the sisters' devotion was a magnificent sight. There they were, kneeling in their gorgeous chapel, wearing their full habits and long white church cloaks."

I took a moment to appraise her. Here was another nun like Mother James, who knew her vocation before she knew how to add and subtract. What was it about the women of this generation that they were sure about what they wanted to do with their lives so early, while many of my contemporaries still don't know? Some of it must have to do with the fact that becoming a nun set women apart from the world of men and even that of ordinary child-rearing, button-saving, meatloaf-cooking women: they became almost another order of being. It was also a way for an ordinary girl to get out in the world, away from the old neighborhoods and their humble roots, and have some authority in schools and hospitals and missions far from home. Girls and women have so many more choices now, although when I mentioned this to Sister Maria later, she reared back and snorted. "There is so much more to *distract* people from this way of life," she said, emphasizing the distinction.

I remembered again those long-ago moments when I wanted to be a nun. I would feel a kind of stunned ecstasy during mass, as if I were shooting skyward in a beam of light. When I left church, I floated to the family car. I'd be tempted to call this rapture now if the word hadn't been trashed by all those bumper stickers on old Chevies reading "Warning! In case of rapture this car will be without a driver." But these were brief, fleeting impulses that quickly gave way to the more enduring passions of my childhood: horses, fighting with the boys, excavating anthills, collecting rocks, creating fairy trails in the woods, and reading about children who fell into fantasy worlds. By the time I was in sixth grade, going to church was merely a tedious social event that I hadn't yet learned to wiggle away from. My friends and I imagined ourselves to be spies during the mass—spies from wild, pagan childhood—using secret gestures or emitting a sequence of chirps to signal that we were aware of each other, that we were not quite under our parents' control. The trick was to do all this so that our families didn't notice and elbow us in front of the righteous.

Aside from the strain of being quiet for an hour, I didn't really object to the mass. I didn't even object to Catholic school except for the fact that my uniform made me stand out in other parts of town, prompting public-school bullies to sneer things like "Catholic Creep" when I walked by. The hard thing was coming up with a suitably scathing response; once I sputtered "Protestant Punks" at them, but this only gave them something more to laugh about. By the time I was in seventh grade, I had convinced my parents to let me leave Catholic school in order to get away from a mean best friend. By the time I finished high school, a philosophy teacher pulled the plug on religion by airing the concept that man had created God, rather than vice versa. It made sense because by then I wanted it to make sense. It was convenient, given that I wanted to skip church on Sundays and mouth off to my mother and sin in as many other ways as I could.

But Sister Maria never lost that first-grade impulse. For her, the feeling for the consecrated life never went away. She also had another secret desire, but this was the flower she kept hidden for decades. One day when she was in her sixth-grade English class, she played a common schoolgirl trick on her English teacher. While the teacher was diagramming sentences on the blackboard at the front of the class, the young Mary Jane was reading something that had nothing to do with English grammar. Not *Lady Chatterley's Lover.* Not *Anna Karenina* or *Madame Bovary* or even *The Wizard of Oz.* Hidden behind the raised top of her desk was a book about the different orders of nuns. When she read the description of the Poor Clares, she made her decision: someday, she would be a Poor Clare.

When I asked what was so appealing about them, Sister Maria brought her finger down on the enclosure wall and tapped out her response. "They were the strictest order. I told myself that was for me."

"Why?"

"I loved my family very much," she said. "I didn't have any attraction to material things—never did—but I really loved my family. I knew that if I was going to give up my life with them I wouldn't go halfway. It would be everything or nothing."

"But it took you such a long time to become a Poor Clare."

She appraised me this time, looking for a moment like a wise infant with her round cheeks and bright eyes and hair tucked under her veil. "This was a grace. If the Lord hadn't put the thought in me, it wouldn't be there. And it wouldn't have stayed there for all those years."

It would take four decades for Sister Maria to make good on this decision. There was an obstacle: in the 1940s, most contemplative orders required that new members arrive with a dowry of $1,000. It was a practical matter as well as an extension of the concept of nuns as brides of Christ, in which they took their vows wearing wedding dresses and holding bouquets of flowers. Interest from the dowry was supposed to support them as they pursued their mission of prayer—and unlike the teaching and nursing of active vocations, prayer was mostly unremunerated. Sister Maria's family didn't have that kind of money. She knew the parish priest did and would be happy to sponsor her, but she didn't want to shame her family by asking for a handout. So instead of looking around for a Poor Clares monastery with an opening, she stayed close to home with the Sisters of the Blessed Sacrament. She began high school there at the age of fifteen, started her years of training for religious life four years later, made her first vows in three years and her perpetual vows after another five years, in 1951. "I was completely happy at the motherhouse," she said with great warmth. "It was truly a second home—and my high school, college, and teacher-training school. I loved those sisters dearly."

Sister Maria was also happy when she left the motherhouse to work in the missions. While she spent time in various places—always working with either poor black or Native American children—she was most animated in her memories of a tiny community called Carencro, in Louisiana. Her students were all the children of black sharecroppers there, and even the children worked terribly hard. They arrived at school after an early morning on the plantation, deposited by a truck meant to carry cotton. Even though the families were poor, the sisters charged tuition—just a dollar—so that the children knew their education had value. The families brought the dollar to the school in their hands, all nickels and pennies and dimes. And at Christmas, the only gifts the children would receive came from the nuns: boxes of candy and pieces of fruit.

Another memory pushed that one aside, and Sister Maria's face shifted quickly from compassion to disgust. "The plantation owners had a general store right there on the grounds," she said. "It was the only place where the black people could buy their food and the other things they needed. So all their money went back to the owners. I tell you, it was terrible." From the look on her face, I imagined that it must have alarmed the plantation owners to see Sister Maria storming up the country roads toward their verandas, her long black veil fluttering like a superhero's cape.

In the middle of our conversation, I realized that I felt more comfortable talking with Sister Maria than I had with the other Poor Clares, less like I was trampling on otherworldly soil. I think that it was because she had been a teaching nun—something familiar to me.

Not too long ago a friend of mine was recounting some horror story from her Catholic school days. "Those teaching nuns had a mean streak," she said with a grimace, feeling again the pincer grip that dragged her from the playground one day. But I liked the nuns at St. Thomas and, by extension, felt friendly toward all nuns. My first-grade teacher was a young, chamois-skinned nun named Sister Cepheus. She had lovely dark eyes but that didn't stop us from being terrified of her for the first few weeks. My first memory of school is of Sister Cepheus walking around the classroom, tapping her wooden pointer on letters of the alphabet that were mounted over the blackboards; my attention, however, was on a small rivulet of pee from a trembling boy in the front of the room as it wound its way down the aisle toward my shoes. My second memory might have been from that same day: I stood outside during recess and held my breath as a pale, acne-scarred nun named Sister Boniface strode past, menacing a group of boys by whacking a wire hanger against her black-draped thigh. But it turned out that they were both kind. Sister Boniface was also a whiz at kickball.

Sister Maria didn't remind me of these two. She made me think of their superior, an imposing woman who cleared hallways as she marched along but regarded the students with an amused rather than stern countenance. I don't remember her name, probably because it was something ordinary like Mary instead of something weird like Cepheus. For a short period of time, I took piano lessons from her. We'd sit together on the piano bench and I'd become silly with the bliss that children get from having an adult pay close attention to them. I remember collapsing with laughter against her ample shoulder when a fly landed on middle C. She was indulgent and didn't pinch my fingers like the next, non-nun piano teacher.

Maybe I was a backward kid, but I didn't have any bizarre fantasies about the St. Thomas nuns' lives. They lived in a big white house next to the school. The windows shone like pools of light. The house hadn't always been there: my father had donated it to the nuns, uprooting it from a lot farther downtown that he hoped would be commercially successful but never was. I remember lining up with the whole town to watch the house being trucked down to Bird Street. The telephone wires were unstrung to let the house pass and there were oohs and aahs as it barely cleared fire hydrants and streetlamps along the way. The only thing I spent any time speculating about was what the nuns looked like when they went to bed. I couldn't imagine what lay underneath the black veil and starched white wimple that framed their eyes and cheeks. Singed patchy hair like the kid I had stared at in kindergarten who had ringworm? Complete baldness? My friends and I discussed this at length.

Remembering all this, hearing Sister Maria talk about her students, it was hard not to think of her departure from an active vocation as a loss. I thought she would have been a wonderful teacher, the kind people recall years later as the guide at a critical turning point in their lives. I imagined a gasp of dismay when she announced her decision to become a contemplative. Her family certainly wasn't happy—she confirmed this—although the comment that she repeated had little to do with spiritual direction. "That's stupid, Mary," a sister-in-law had said. "I won't give you a day in there because you can't keep your mouth shut, even in a place like that."

But Sister Maria's desire to become a Poor Clare was reactivated when her father died in 1975. She said she was so forlorn that she nearly wanted to climb in the grave with him. One day, she became too depressed to work among the other nuns and went to her room. She began talking to her father as if he were sitting next to her. "I told him I always wanted to be a Poor Clare," she said to me, then dropped her voice a notch. "I didn't tell him that I never went that way because of the money. And I told him, if you're in heaven could you please tell our Lord? I couldn't see how I could do this—it would mean leaving the Sisters of the Blessed Sacrament. But I knew that if God wanted me in the Poor Clares, there was nothing that could stop his hand."

"And?" I asked. "And then what?"

"Then you wouldn't believe what happened," she said, settling back in her chair and giving me a wink.

A year after her father's death, Sister Maria accompanied a friend to Washington, DC. There was a terrible storm, but she waded out into the hip-deep snow to meet a young man who was studying for the priesthood and had promised to take her to a special shrine. She knelt down to pray at the shrine, which was a replica of one in Jerusalem that is dedicated to Christ's passion in the garden. Suddenly, it seemed that a message came to her: "Do my will as you see me doing the will of my father."

As she repeated the message to me, Sister Maria looked almost as disgusted as when she had talked about the plantation owners. She glared at one of the bars on the grate between us. "I stood there and said, 'Well, Lord, I didn't have to come all the way to DC to hear that! I could've read that in any old spiritual book back home.'"

Then she started to feel ashamed of herself for taking that tone with God. She almost didn't hear her friend ask if she wanted to stop at the Poor Clares' monastery, which was just down the street. However, she followed his directions and visited the monastery for an hour of prayer. After she finished, she called one of the community's externs to unlock the monastery door so that she could fight her way through the storm before night fell. But instead of opening the door right away, the extern stood and peered at her. "Out of the clear blue sky, she asks if I want to be a Poor Clare!" Sister Maria whispered. "And she started saying things to me that only God and I know."

We were silent for a few seconds. This was the moment

in her past when the bolts to the door of her desire started slip-
ping away, and she seemed to want to savor it.

"Then what?" I finally urged.

"I told her that she had to be kidding. I was almost fifty
years old! And she says back to me, 'When God calls, it makes
no difference.'"

Sister Maria took the vocation materials the extern
offered just to humor her, but spent many days studying them.
She wanted to see if there was anything in the order's rules that
would keep her from entering. There wasn't. "After that the
desire was just pouring into me, Kris," Sister Maria said. "I told
my priest in confession and then went to see my superior. She
didn't want to let me go, but I told her that when my day comes
to answer to God she won't be there with me—I'll have to
answer for myself. And she let me go."

She looked at her hands, then back up at me. "I tell you,
Kris, the Lord has me spooked. I can't believe he's given me all
this."

When we had started the interview at 9:00, Sister Maria
had told me she didn't know how useful she'd be—that she
didn't have much to say. However, the woman was bursting
with words: my two hours were almost up and there hadn't
been one awkward silence. Now, I could hear the rest of the sisters singing somewhere in the monastery: Kenny the organist
was teaching them some new pieces for the Easter season and
their voices were sounding sweeter than ever. I knew I had only
a few more minutes with Sister Maria.

"Did you miss anything when you came inside?" I asked.
"You led such an active life before—you traveled, you taught all

those children, you were part of their family life—don't you miss that?"

She smiled. "I miss driving in the country. I miss certain friends. But so many people write and I just can't keep up with them. We're not allowed that kind of correspondence."

She explained that contact of any kind was restricted. Even with family and friends, she was only allowed to write a letter or visit with them in this parlor once every two months. I was taken aback by this news: I had thought that their rules of enclosure mandated only the wall and grates, not the number of times the Poor Clares were able to have human contact. Given that, I suddenly realized that it was remarkable that the sisters had agreed to meet with me weekly. It was also alarming, as I realized that this visit with the seemingly indomitable Sister Maria was probably my last.

I must have been frowning, which I often do while thinking things through—my mother still flicks me on the forehead when I do it and warns me about wrinkles. But Sister Maria must have thought that I was disturbed to hear about the severity of their isolation. "People only see the outside of our lives," she said gently. "It can look very negative to them but it's the 'why' that makes the difference. We don't live like this to punish ourselves but to have a deeper prayer life. If you're not seeking a deep relationship with God, then none of this makes any sense."

I thought again about her work in Carencro, imagined her greeting the children who were eager to come to school from a daybreak stint in the cotton fields. I asked if some people thought she was making a mistake to leave all that good work behind. Even though I had to ask, this seemed like nitpicking; I was awed by her deep satisfaction with this life. It was easy to imagine her rush of feeling when she swept into the Poor Clares cloister for the first time, as if she were returning to a home she had never actually seen but had yearned for over the course of decades. It clearly hadn't disappointed her, this escape from the clamorous outside world in which God's voice was only one of many.

"Some people think this is a big waste of time." She leaned forward to put her elbow on the wall and spoke again in a confidential tone. "You have to have deep faith for our kind of life because you have nothing to show for it. In an active community, you see the results. We don't see the results. We have to let God take care of them. All we can do is enrich our prayer life. The richer it is, the more fruitful it will be for the people who ask for our help."

Sister Maria stood and shook the folds from her habit. She laughed ruefully when she saw me stretch my hand and rub the spot where my pen had dented my finger, then she waved and left the room. I pondered the Sister Maria paradox all the way home. The thing was, I could imagine her striding along so many other paths in life. I could imagine her taking Madeline Albright and then Colin Powell's place if Bosnia and Serbia and all those other fractious places get too hard to handle. I could imagine her running a saloon, planting that emphatic elbow on the bar and trading stories with customers, pitching drunks into the street as easily as she brushed the lint from her habit. If one of the cracks in the parlor wall split and the entire building started to come down, I could imagine Sister Maria reaching up to hold everything in place, her cheeks puffing with exertion. And I thought it remarkable that of all the nuns I had met, it was only the doughty Sister Maria who had been inspired by the example of the frail and sickly Clare.

But was it inspiration or compulsion? Sister Maria's story also fascinated me because she continued to want this life decade after decade, even though she was doing something else that she loved. She never stopped hearing God's siren call—as maybe I had heard it, for a few moments, back when I was six years old—and it continued to tug at her over the years. Perhaps some people *are* chosen for this, I thought. That was certainly what the nuns believed, and it might be the reason they didn't get terribly discouraged as their ranks dwindled. Maybe it was possible to see this as a choice God was making, that he had more pressing tasks for his other beloveds and would restock the contemplative shelves as he saw fit.

At least a few of the people at the shrine felt that God had chosen to lead me to the nuns and had kindled my desire to write about them. This was an unnerving suggestion. It made me feel erroneously ennobled, since I knew that a yearning for faith was only part of what tugged me toward the shrine. I was also drawn by plain nosiness combined with the notion that I might wreak a salable book from my visits, plus the pleasure of talking with these mysterious women when most other people couldn't. Still, some people insisted otherwise, even with my disclaimers. Once I hung around the shrine after a big Saturday function, helping a group of parishioners wipe down the tables in the Guild Room and pick up plastic cups. Sister Regina and Sister Claire Marie, the two extern Poor Clares, were also helping out. I hadn't seen Sister Claire Marie since the day I had entered the cloister with the newspaper photographer. As the two of us stacked folding chairs in a closet, she said, "It's Kris, isn't it? I see you sitting in the same place in church on Sundays, but you look a little different today." She was being polite as well as judicious: I looked extraordinarily different, since I had told my hair guy to do whatever he wanted and was punished with what looked like golden retriever ears on the sides of my head. He and I went through this routine fairly often. If the nuns watched my Sunday-morning spot with any regularity, they must have been confused by the kaleidoscope of colors and shapes on my head.

But when I mentioned Sister Claire Marie's words to the ever-present Lynn, she opened her eyes wide. "That's a sign," she said. "It's very special when one of God's chosen notices you." I tried to explain that I had met Sister Claire Marie when I was accompanying the newspaper photographer inside the cloister and that she was just being courteous. Lynn would have none of it.

6

*E*ach time I interviewed one of the Poor Clares, I was surprised by how different she was from the others.

It wasn't just the varied accents, although they were striking: Mother James, Sister Thomas, Sister Regina, and Sister Maria all spoke English so differently that if I had met them elsewhere I would assume they had never lived within five hundred miles of each other. I don't live in the same house with my girlfriends, but we've still borrowed each other's regional speech—I've added Francine's flat Cleveland a's and Susan's intriguing Long Island s's to my small-town California inflection, and I still say "Jeez Louise" sometimes, even though my friend Andi moved to Chicago seven years ago. But the nuns not only kept their accents separate: they shared no idioms, no mannerisms, they didn't even seem to share relevant news. Sister Thomas didn't know about the Poor Clares Web site that I'd helped Mother James put together. Sister Maria had been on hand for part of the drama of Sister Anne Marie's death—she was downstairs when the EMS pounded on the doors of the church and saw Mother James come flying down the stairs to let them in. Otherwise, I got the impression she might not have known any of the details. Since these women had lived together in the same house for decades, I had expected them to have fused into a group personality, a sort of undifferentiated mass of brown serge. This was hardly the case.

When I returned to the blue parlor the week after my interview with Sister Maria, yet another distinct personality was waiting for me. Actually, she was not waiting for me—no one was there, and the basket-weave wooden screen that was usually folded against the wall was stretched across the grates. Anne peeked in a few times to see if anyone had come, then I could hear her paging Mother James on the intercom system for what seemed like ten minutes. Finally, there was the sound of someone running along a hall. I heard the door on the nuns' side of the parlor creak open. Pretty soon a hand appeared at the side of the screen and then a very short nun, who wrestled the screen to the wall. She was panting from her run. Before she dropped into her chair, she stopped to adjust a pair of glasses that had wide, square lenses about as big as her cheeks. "I'm Sister Bernadette," she said, and wrinkled her nose. "I forgot."

This was another thing that intrigued me about the nuns: while they were always warm and gracious as they greeted me in the parlor, I didn't get the feeling that they were eagerly awaiting my visits. Sister Bernadette was not the first to forget an interview. I don't think I'm terribly bloated with pride—maybe just a bit puffy around the eyes—but I figured that the nuns would consider a visit from me or *anyone* special enough to remember. It's not that they had no other visitors. A devoted core hung around the shrine: Lynn; Kenny the organist and his tiny, ancient mother and aunt; the older black man who had pulled me into the shrine's aegis by handing me the collection basket on that first Christmas morning—I now knew him as Artemus—and the other regulars who visited the shrine often, even daily, and sometimes requested special visits with one of the sisters. And it's not that I was their only new visitor. As with any group, there were changes among the group that I had dubbed the "regulars." The black-browed woman and the pale, face-of-a-saint woman had disappeared. Others had taken their places, including three tall, craggy brothers—two wore leather cowboy hats that made them look as if they had just arrived from the Australian outback—who began turning up every Sunday. One of them always made one cheesecake to serve in the Guild Room after Sunday mass and one for Sister Regina to carry back into the cloister. Even though I had been introduced several times, I couldn't think of them as anything but the "Cheesecake Brothers." Whenever I referred to them this way, the other regulars knew immediately who I meant.

Still, I think I was the only regular visitor who had tumbled so far from Catholicism that I was a virtual stranger to the church. And I knew from my research that this group of Poor Clares had been largely forgotten for years, even by area Catholics. They had also evaded the hungry gaze of the local media, which might logically be on the lookout for a human-interest piece about a group of downtown nuns who viewed life through a series of grates. When I was working on the article for the *Plain Dealer Sunday Magazine*, the newspaper archivist had searched their files for news of the nuns. Articles were few and

far between: a short piece in the religion section four years earlier when these nuns celebrated the seventy-fifth anniversary of
their arrival in Cleveland; a two-inch piece about the illness of
the community's founder, Mother Mary Agnes, in 1962; and a
handful of short articles from the late 1930s about the then-
annual Street of Nations fair held outside the shrine, at which
hundreds of volunteers sold handicrafts to raise money for the
nuns. It was true that the nuns had received more attention
since my article was published and were even featured in a short
television segment. After one of the nuns greeted me by saying,
"Are you the reporter who's collecting stories about miracles?"
I started to wonder if maybe they were on media overload.

But Sister Bernadette didn't seem as if she had been
dreading the prospect of speaking to another reporter. As she
caught her breath, she regarded me with bright, curious eyes
and gave the screen an extra push. "We use this for confession,"
she said. "The priest was in here last night and the last person
forgot to fold it away." Then she wiggled to the front of her
chair, folded her arms, and leaned comfortably on the ledge. It
was just the right height for her.

"I'm not a very spontaneous person," she said as I looked
down my list of questions. "I don't know if I can answer all those."

This was one thing the nuns seemed to have in common: they didn't think they'd have anything interesting to say to
their Friday-morning inquisitor. "Here's an easy question," I
said. "When did you become a Poor Clare?"

"In 1955." She watched with amusement as I processed
the number in my head. "That makes forty-five years."

"Did you always know you wanted to be a nun?"

Sister Bernadette shook her head vigorously. "I never even thought of it until one day when I went to confession here at the shrine. The priest asked if I'd ever considered becoming a nun, and I told him yes, but I really hadn't. Then after he said that, I got to thinking. I felt that I wanted something more from life. I wanted to make something of it and going to God could be that thing."

Like Sister Thomas, she had been thoroughly immersed in a happy and active life on the outside—it wasn't nearly as exotic as Sister Thomas's life, but it had many simple pleasures. She explained that she grew up only a few blocks away from St. Paul Shrine with four sisters and two brothers, one of whom still lives in the old, now-run-down neighborhood. She had many friends and a job she enjoyed in the secretarial pool at a farm-equipment manufacturing company. One of her brothers would get tickets to the Cleveland Indians baseball games from time to time, and in 1948, along with 80,000 other fans, the two of them attended the last World Series that the Cleveland team won. She still follows the team's fortunes—she's the Poor Clare who dives for the sports page every day. She sometimes watches the lights of Jacobs Field from the monastery's rooftop garden, and when she's lying in bed at night she can hear the fireworks after one of the players hits a home run or the riotous series of explosions when the team wins a game. It still thrills her, even though she hasn't seen a game or even heard one on the radio for nearly five decades.

But the priest's words awakened a longing that she thinks was buried deep inside. She remembered reading a booklet describing contemplative communities back in eighth grade. "It said that if you liked the moments after communion and the benediction, this might be the life for you," she told me.

"Why those moments?"

"You draw closer to him in those moments," she said, looking amused again. I was trying to remember what exactly the benediction was and was probably making a face. "Your contact with the Lord is special in those moments."

Her family was happy about her decision, but leaving them turned out to be harder than she had thought. Her father died just before she was scheduled to enter and her mother panicked and didn't want her to leave. But Sister Bernadette felt there were enough members of the family to help her mother through this time, and she was afraid she wouldn't fulfill her desire for the consecrated life if she waited for the crisis to pass.

When she entered the Poor Clares' monastery, she was twenty-three years old and had been caught up in studies of Carmelite hermits—in fact, she had even applied for admission to a Carmelite monastery and was turned away because the prioress thought the life might be too strict for her there. So her difficulty in adjusting to monastic life was not what I would have expected: instead of finding it too isolating, she struggled to become comfortable living with so many other women. The Poor Clares spent most of their time together—at prayer, at meals, at their various chores—rather than in solitary contemplation. Since Sister Bernadette had steeped herself in the stories of hermits and all their marvelous deprivations, that took some getting used to.

So it is a little like a commune, I thought while listening to her describe this world of women living and working together. A tiny pang shook me as I thought about how well this kind of life—minus the celibacy and the vocation—would suit me. I've always loved living within a constellation of people, probably because I pined for that kind of enveloping familiarity when I was a kid. My own family was both big and small: big because I had four brothers and sisters; small because they had all left the house by the time I was six. My father was traveling a lot and my mother developed an illness that kept her confined; our home was then silent and still. When my siblings came back for the holidays, I leaped around them like a small dog. I danced on their shoes. I kept myself from falling asleep at night just so I could lie in my bed and listen to the sound of them: voices, laughter, footsteps, odd thumps and crashes, the popcorn popper in the kitchen, the doors opening and closing. And it was even more wonderful when my mother's sister and her family came to visit. There were six Metzker children, and I was younger than even the youngest of them, but not by much; when they'd come for a visit I'd start waiting for them early in the morning, an eager, sentient stone at the side of the road. I went on to love college dorms, and the crowded student hovels that I moved into after the dorms, and even the creaking old apartment building that I lived in when I was first married, in which other people's racket transgressed the walls. When my daughter comes home from college and I wake in the middle of the night to hear her and her friends engaged in some kind of hushed hilarity in the living room, I roll over in bliss.

Sister Bernadette's account of their life puzzled me, though. If they spent so much time together, why did each of them remain so distinct, so close to who they were before they entered, and so meagerly possessed of gossip? I thought that even the most trivial news would circulate faster than the flu in this tiny community, where the activities of each day varied so little from the day before. The answer surfaced without my even having to ask the question. Sister Bernadette was telling me about their three-quarters hour of recreation every evening. "Yes." I nodded. "One of the other sisters was telling me that some of you play cards."

"Or we just talk," she said. "All the rest of the day is spent in silence, so sometimes it's nice just to talk."

"I didn't know you kept silence all day!" I probably shouldn't have been surprised, since I knew that some orders do maintain silence much of the time and I'd never heard any talking outside the Poor Clares' parlor. I guess I had assumed that the building was so big and the walls were so thick that the noise of any chatter was absorbed before it could reach my ears. "You talk to each other at meals, don't you?"

Sister Bernadette shook her head. "We usually listen to religious tapes at meals. On a sister's feast day and on her birthday and all during the Christmas season and on some other national holidays there is talking at meals. But the rest of the time we observe silence."

"You say absolutely nothing to each other all day except for during those forty-five minutes?"

She moved her hands apart, as if showing how the rules could be stretched. "It's not as strict as it used to be. When I first came, the sisters wrote little notes to each other if they needed something during the day. Now, we can converse about what we need. We can also go off to a room together if we need to talk about something serious. But the rest of the time we remain silent."

"Are you praying or thinking about something special during the silence?"

"We all have jobs here, and we think about that," she said, smiling again. "But for the most part, we're trying to be centered on the Lord. Our life is very intense that way."

So that was it. Before I started to meet with the nuns, I had imagined their life as a kind of spiritual quilting bee where they spent their days gabbing about theology, the lives of the saints, and their letters from home. Now, I was starting to understand the effect of their vocation: they shared a life, but it wasn't one that allowed them to develop the kind of intimacy that most people in such close quarters share. There wasn't a lot of back-and-forth between them, and even though they pondered the same spiritual mysteries they were freed by their workaday silence and their solitary hours of prayer to ponder them in their own way. Each had a unique approach to adoration—in fact, Sister Bernadette told me that she sang to God during her adoration hours. Theirs was a company of solitary seekers: they were pilgrims wandering in search of God, so absorbed by their pursuit, so removed from the physical world by their preoccupation with spirit, and so atomized by the vastness of the divine that they hardly bumped into each other. No wonder they hadn't lost their accents, no wonder they didn't know that much about each other. No wonder they seemed without guile—there was no one for them to fool. For twenty-three and a quarter hours of the day, they were alone with their own voices. Sometimes they were also with God, in the sense that they felt his presence. But not always, Sister Bernadette said, echoing something Sister Thomas had told me months before: the point of their life was not this feeling, however much it is cherished, but faithfulness. The feeling of closeness to God is a special grace, she said, and it can even elude one of them for most of a lifetime. Faithfulness is the choice made every day, and only they and God know whether or not they make it.

"Maybe I shouldn't be revealing this." Sister Bernadette winced a little, even as she continued to smile. "For me this is mostly a life of faith. I continue living the life, even if I feel sometimes that I'm just going through the motions."

How brave, I thought, how steadfast and strong, noting even as I thought it that my reaction would have been the opposite a decade ago: how foolish, I would have gasped, how deluded and pathetic! Unlike active religious communities, the Poor Clares' entire lives were centered around their divine husband. They had given up everything for him—their families, their friends, their money, the lush and beautiful earth that God's other creatures were free to frolic across with little heed of a creator. Most women would consider this the marriage from hell. There is no sex, the husband doesn't help support the household—he won't even fix a broken light switch or check the mousetraps or hand tools to the plumber—and there can be no expectation of emotional intimacy. No matter how loyal they are, no matter how they try to please this husband, the nuns cannot assume that they will hear his steady loving voice, even in their darkest moments. He might be listening to them, his heart might ache for them, but who can tell?

So why do I now find this devotion admirable rather than stupid? I guess I'm tired of a world with so little faith. I'm tired of marriages that fall apart because people won't persevere through the dry, dull, miserable periods; I'm tired of people who have given up on making the world better; I'm tired of people who cynically deconstruct everything for their own amusement—and I've been all these people. These nuns fell in love with God, married him after a long, careful courtship, and have stuck with him year after year. Looking at Sister Bernadette's reassuring smile—I felt she weighed telling me about her struggle to feel close to God for fear of discomfiting me—I was dazzled by the strength of her commitment.

And I was intrigued that she struggled along this daily path of faith without an ongoing dialogue with the other nuns urging her along. How different from life in the outside world, where we talk about everything. We can't imagine intimacy without words, without discussing the history and the shape and the terms of our feelings. At least, this is the way I am: I've called friends from phones outside gas stations four hundred miles from home, called them with cars raising a gritty wind on nearby roads to relieve a sudden clutch of loneliness. As I was writing this chapter, I got a phone call late at night from the son of a woman I hardly knew; she and I had worked together on a writing-related project. His mother had died the day before, the man told me, and he had been going through her Rolodex and e-mails trying to determine whom he needed to tell. I guess I have terrible manners, because I asked right away how she died and then wished I hadn't: she had committed suicide. All I could do was cry about her for two days—I'm crying as I write this now—and I told everyone I saw or corresponded with about her. How I had seen her for the first time in months at the grocery store a few weeks before and she had told me she'd been having a hard time. How I had been friendly but not aggressively kind. How I had not taken her arm right then and insisted that we have a cup of coffee together, how I hadn't brought her home for dinner, how I hadn't tucked her into the bed in my daughter's unused room and covered her with a flannel quilt. I knew she was a ship with many holes and I don't know what might have kept her above water, but I wished I had done more than send her a cheery e-mail on the day I last saw her. The worst was when I imagined her picking her spot, uncorking the bottle of pills, plodding methodically toward death in all her terrible pain and grief. I cried and I talked to one friend after another and in the middle of it all, I prayed that God would catch her gently as she fell from this life and hold her in his arms and relieve her of all pain. This was not the kind of prayer I had to pinch myself to remember: I was compelled toward it. I wanted to be like one of the anguished supplicants that I sometimes see at the shrine, alone in its dark pews— begging, weeping, sucking in mercy.

The Poor Clares tell God these things and spare themselves the distraction of human voices. While they indulge in some conversation, their way of life means that they know each other mainly from the outside—from the way they actually behave—and their shared purpose. I think each of us has two selves—the outside self that others see and that we don't, and the inner self, the one we're always trying to reveal to each other. Somehow we've become convinced that the inner self is the one that's real, while the outer self is only a facade. After having any number of people tell me who they think I am while I know a very different person on the inside, I've decided that maybe the reverse is true. It's the outer self that gets us through the world even when we don't feel we can manage it, persevering through class reunions and first dates and vicious days at work despite the tyrannical bleating of the inner self. Maybe we reinforce our fears by speaking of them too much. Maybe these Poor Clares are able to carry on because a certain amount of silence keeps doubt in its place.

Of course, by the time I met Sister Bernadette there was a lot more silence in the Poor Clares' monastery than there used to be. When she entered in 1955, she was yet another young woman in a lively group of postulants who clumped and chattered their way around a monastery. There was more togetherness and animated conversation among the postulants than among the older nuns, and they studied together, prayed together, and took lessons together. They were *girls* together, embarking upon something exciting and new. I had already read something of this youthful vigor in the book Mother James had given me so many months before. She was right: I did love *A Right to Be Merry*, which was written in the early 1950s by Mother Mary Francis, a young poet-turned-nun from an order called the Poor Clares of the Colettine reform. The book reminded me a little of *Anne of Green Gables* and all the books that followed; it shared the high spirits and earnestness of those books and made me feel—as the Anne books did when I was a girl—that there used to be more people with a kind of homespun nobility to them. Not to imply that *A Right to Be Merry* is

preachy: Mother Mary Francis was a fine, surprising writer and
I found her book charming.

But hers had been a young voice back then, writing
about a cloistered community rocked by the exuberance of
young women. She herself was so anxious that she might fall
short of the Poor Clare ideal when she entered that she could
scarcely eat. She was often ambushed by fits of napping during
daytime prayer because she could barely sleep at night. Her
teeth chattered when it was her turn to chant a lesson in front
of the other sisters. She shouted prayers instead of just reading
them. And she was not alone in her coltish, heart-thumping
pursuit of the spiritual life. From the perspective of just a few
years in the monastery, she wrote fondly of those even newer
girls who came in after her:

> *Postulants are young, religious creatures who laugh at
> everything and often at nothing. They giggle in moments of
> silent solemnity. They have a rare talent for making much
> noise in quiet cloisters, but themselves hearing none of it.
> They wear black uniforms and thin, black veils, looking from
> the back like demure young widows and from the front like
> anything else but that. They sing Gregorian chant not very
> well but very loud, and chant the Divine Office in bright,
> metallic voices—when they can find the place in the fat bre-
> viary whose spray of colored ribbon markers they daily
> entangle in the most intricate knots and loops.*

What a contrast with the silent monastery of *my* Poor Clares,
where the sound of Anne's grandchildren playing in the dark

entryway was the only sign of youth. And what a contrast to the community Sister Bernadette entered forty-five years ago.

Still, only Mother James seemed to worry about whether new vocations, as they called them, would come knocking at the door—or begin hitting their Internet site. She had told me that there were still Poor Clare monasteries that drew substantial numbers of young girls, and I could hear the longing and heartbreak in her voice. It seemed to be the celebrity abbesses that attracted vocations. Mother Angelica, television nun, drew many donation dollars, built a marvelous new shrine of white marble down in Alabama, and, according to Mother James, had new members streaming in the door. Mother Mary Francis was also somewhat of a celebrity abbess now, managing a desert monastery in New Mexico that had so much vigor that her community opened a new house in Holland and was getting ready to open still another in Chicago. Mother Francis continued to make a name for the Poor Clares by writing books, plays, and poems from the cloister and had even loaded the Internet with several pieces. She hadn't lost her deft touch with words in her more than fifty years behind the grates. She also didn't seem to have lost touch with the ways of the outside world, as this recruitment newsletter written in tongue-in-cheek advertising hyperbole showed:

Do the words MY GOD AND MY ALL say it all for you?

Then don't delay to take full advantage of this ONCE-IN-A-LIFETIME-FOR-AS-LONG-AS-YOUR-LIFETIME offer awaiting you in our little desert monastery, where a blessed life for God features a life of. . . . HARD LABOR!

That's right! Here is your chance to serve God with that full enthusiasm of mind and body bequeathed to us in our Franciscan way. If you have ever secretly supposed the contemplative life to be a leisurely round of devotional exercises, punctuated by strolls in the garden and a spot of embroidery now and again, FEAR NO MORE! You will be relieved to know that for the cloistered nun, loving God demands full-time spiritual, mental and physical elbow grease. . . .

If I were one of the Cleveland Poor Clares watching as more and more parts of the monastery's old living area were turned into storage space, I think I'd feel abandoned. Worse, I'd feel that the dwindling numbers were an indictment of the choice I had made. If so few people persisted in this way of life, I'd wonder if all my years away from the world were in vain, if my faith may just have been wistfulness after all, if all those others who were staying away knew some bitter truth I couldn't accept.

The emptying of the cloister happened so gradually that it hardly seemed like a trend. "Every room used to be full," Sister Bernadette told me, her small frame rocking precariously on the edge of her chair. "It was nice, it was a close community. Every year, we had a big cleaning and each sister was assigned to a portion of the monastery and we'd do it all. Now, that's impossible. People die, people leave, and before you really know it there's just a few of us left."

S he's a beautiful woman," Mother James murmured in the most reverent of tones. "Very tall, very graceful even now that she's in her seventies."

I had just told Mother James that I was reading *A Right to Be Merry*. She was telling me about the time she met Mother Mary Francis, who came to Cleveland for a meeting at the monastery of the Poor Clares of the Colettine reform in Rocky River, a suburb to the west of Cleveland. It seems that Cleveland has always been a hotbed of Poor Clares activity. They started showing up here in 1826 and there are now three groups: Mother James's Poor Clares of Perpetual Adoration downtown, the Colettines, and another called the Poor Clares of the Byzantine Rite. They have almost nothing to do with each other, though, and Mother James wouldn't ordinarily recruit someone to drive her all the way out to Rocky River. Still, she'd heard through the grapevine that the greatly admired Mother Mary Francis would be in town.

The two abbesses talked for a short while. Mother James

didn't tell me the details of their conversation—for all I know, they may have discussed quirky quotidian matters such as how to dissuade Sister X from humming when she peels the potatoes because it drives Sister Y crazy. But what struck me about Mother James's recollection was her rapt attention to the other nun's beauty. Her admiration had an almost spiritual quality to it, as if a beautiful face and figure were the natural outgrowth of a beautiful soul. As if the quality of one's devotion to God shaped you from the inside out. I found this attention to physical beauty odd, then remembered Clare of Assisi. After all, Mother James and the others were walking in her footsteps. By every account, they were beautiful feet.

Eight hundred years after her death, Clare remains a fascinating woman. To the hundreds of thousands of people who pay attention to saints and their putative powers, she represents spiritual tenacity, almost to the point of rebellion. Her determination to lead a life of poverty nearly drove a series of popes to distraction. On her deathbed, she finally received Pope Innocent IV's approval of her rule, which—alarming for the times—included an instruction that each of her nuns should "sell all that she has and take care to distribute the proceeds to the poor." She was the first woman in history to have written one of these rules that order the lives of religious communities; she was reportedly so delighted by the pope's acquiescence that she kissed the papal decree over and over even as she was breathing her last. Clare is also an example of how even frail, trembling hands can wield the might of God. She is often depicted standing on a stony parapet, her ailing body buttressed by her nuns, lifting the Blessed Sacrament over her head to drive invaders from her monastery. I'm sure people call on Clare for the blessing of perseverance, for a prayerful advantage in desperate situations, for a spirit of steel when the flesh is but crumbling ash. Then there is the really odd Clare connection. When her nuns left her in her sickbed to attend a Christmas mass, Clare is reported to have had a vision: she said the Lord allowed her to view the mass on the wall of her bedroom. Because she was the first person to receive a live transmission of images from afar, Pope Pius XII declared her the patron saint of television in 1958. I suppose, then, that one could also call on Clare for the strength to click off reruns of *Buffy the Vampire Slayer*.

As I became interested in the Poor Clares—and through them, these odd bits of Catholic lore—I read through some fairly traditional accounts of saintly doings. I didn't much like these accounts. There is so much that is fatuously believed, so much that seems left out, so much that is obviously scripted to bolster the position of the Church, and so much that is just boring. Some writers burnish the lives of Clare and other saints until they're flat; only their spiritual sheen is left behind. Still, even the official story of Clare interests me for what it can't help but admit. It sometimes seems that she's revered for all the wrong reasons—for her supposed docility, for her great serenity, for remaining the luminous shadow of Francis who stayed behind walls instead of roaming the countryside with him. But she had to have been a woman of great passion. No one knows the exact cause of her death, but it probably resulted from years of starvation and self-abuse, which she practiced as a penance. I think of her death as spontaneous combustion, the final self-immolation of a soul on fire.

Clare was the third of five children in a noble family that was at odds with Assisi's rising merchant class. I have always imagined the life of thirteenth-century ladies as castle-bound and tedious, but the women in Clare's family were well educated and her mother, Ortolano, even made a perilous journey to the Holy Land. Ortolano was a pious woman and visited a nearby church often during her third pregnancy, praying anxiously for the baby's health. One day, she is said to have heard a voice say, "O lady, do not be afraid, for you will joyfully bring forth a clear light which will illumine the world." Ortolano and her husband, Favarone, named their baby girl Chiara, or Clare, meaning "the clear one."

Clare was praised for her docility when she was a young girl, but this changed when she met Francis. Already betrothed by her uncle to another nobleman, Clare heard Francis—a former roué and son of a prosperous merchant—preaching in one of Assisi's piazzas and she was smitten by his message of divine love. And Francis was ready to receive her fervor: after his conversion, he had restored the ruined San Damiano church and prophesied that a group of religious women would someday be its occupants. One night in 1212, Clare fled her family home in her bridal finery, choosing the one door that was unguarded—the one that was used to take corpses from the house. Even this door was heavily bolted, but Clare beat against it until locks and beams gave way. She hurried to a secret, prearranged meeting with Francis. Her glowing hair was shorn and then snuffed by dark veils, and she soon moved into San Damiano, where she would stay for the rest of her life. Her sister Agnes joined her in sixteen days. Their uncle was so enraged to lose yet another marriageable asset that he sent a group of men to bring Agnes home. Legend has it that the girl suddenly became so heavy that the men couldn't lift her, and she remained with Clare in the monastery. Eventually, even their mother joined them. Clare spent most of her years in poor health. By the time of her death in 1253, there were 150 monasteries full of Poor Ladies.

When Mother James first told me that Clare had to fight the Church establishment for the privilege of poverty, I didn't understand the nature of the objection—certainly, few people consider poverty a privilege these days. Some traditional Catholic writers have made the issue a little clearer for me. Francis and Clare embraced poverty because Jesus had chosen his life on earth as a poor man, and they wanted to live like him, without assets, tapping humanity's vein of generosity for their living. While there had been a history of itinerant holy men who went about begging and preaching for centuries, there was no such tradition for women. Many cloistered women—and this was the main option for religious women—lived in plush monasteries that had been endowed by princesses or baronesses. It seems that these endowments were statements of one's social position as well as acts of faith, in much the same way that millionaires endow medical buildings and theater lobbies today. These foundresses sometimes held the title of "abbess" but rarely had anything to do with the actual practice of faith going on in the enclosure. Clare was a very different foundress: she wanted nothing to do with her money. She also wanted her ladies to dispense with their own fortunes and embrace poverty, living only on alms from believers and what they could earn with their own hands. I guess it was a privilege to try to live like Jesus, and Clare was pleading to be considered as ascetically fit as men. She was asserting that women didn't need a medieval money-bags standing by to clutter their contemplation with comfort. Even the churchiest of writers allow that Clare kept Francis's dream of Christ-like poverty alive after his death in 1226. In *Francis and Clare: The Complete Works*, Friars Regis Armstrong and Ignatius Brady say:

> *While the friars were accepting papal indults that relaxed their practice of poverty, Clare was courageously clinging to the primitive ideals and challenging the Holy See to allow her and her sisters to maintain the charism of poverty, which she had received from Francis himself. Through this woman, then, the Spirit of the Lord expressed the Franciscan ideal in a pure, brilliant way and confronted and challenged her contemporaries to a serious consideration of its value.*

But Clare's insistence on poverty was more radical still. According to *Sisters in Arms*, Jo Ann Kay McNamara's fascinating and definitive tome on nuns, Francis and Clare weren't the only people in the Middle Ages obsessed with poverty. The wild countryside of Europe had been consumed by farms and villages, and the cities were burgeoning. With all these thousands of people from different classes pressed together in the cities, the differences between the wealthy and the poor had become glaring. McNamara says that for the first time,

> *Europe was beginning to resemble the world where Jesus once walked, giving vivid and passionate reality to the theology of his humanity. The urban patriarchs appeared, seeking to buy nobility by adorning their cities with churches and displaying their prestige by acts of charity. The urban poor also emerged, the "huddled masses" who haunted the consciences of the rich . . . Wandering preachers appeared in marketplaces and public squares, berating the prosperous for their devotion to filthy lucre and their lack of charity for those who fell by the wayside.*

Many people of noble families responded by divesting themselves of their wealth and living a life of poverty. Women were strong within this current: since preaching and so many other religious activities were denied them, they were often eager to give up their inheritances or endowments and either embrace a life of prayer or one of caring for the poor. There seems to have been a loathing among these noblewomen for their own assets. Since they couldn't decide whom to marry on their own anyway—this was decided by parents or, in the case of Clare, her uncle—their wealth could be a burden, attracting cruel and loutish aristocrats as suitors. Their riches were like stones dragging them to the bottom of a chill and noisome lake. By giving up their money or, at least, any future claims to it, these women were in fact cutting away that which forced them into unwanted unions. Again from McNamara:

> *Many women associated control of money with control of their own bodies. They fled from property as they fled from becoming the property of others . . . If we look back to the violence with which some women were herded into marriage, perhaps we can understand the connection of money and rape as joint threats and understand their flight from both. This complicated phenomenon seems to connect purity and poverty, freedom and chastity, rebellion and renunciation.*

This was the sort of women's liberation that was taking place in Clare's time. Fathers and uncles and brothers weren't too keen on this phenomenon, either. Giving up money suggests that you have some right to it, after all—that you have power over it rather than it having power over you. But this is not the way thirteenth-century patriarchs saw it: if a woman had assets because she was widowed or had received an inheritance, it was understood that she was only tending the money until she could use it to enrich her male heirs. McNamara's discussion of thirteenth-century sexual politics makes Clare seem much more likeable to me—more likeably subversive—than even the Church accounts did. It's not that she gave up sex because she found the idea of sex distasteful, it's not that she gave up her fortune because she had some idiotically romantic notion about what it was like to be poor. Or maybe she did find sex distasteful and had idiotically romantic notions about the poor; still, it is clear that taking flight from her riches was one of the few ways that she could exercise any sort of choice in her life. She put a beautiful face on poverty for the ages.

Still, there was some back-and-forth after Clare's death about this issue of poverty. Even though she was quickly proclaimed a saint, church authorities were eager to strip the much-sought privilege of poverty from her order. Within ten years, Pope Urban IV gave a new rule to the Poor Clares allowing them to own communal property. The crack of luxury opened, and many monasteries toppled in. Over the centuries, some of her followers have lived in palatial convents while others lived in cherished wretchedness, inspired by reformers who remained true to Clare's vision. Sometimes, both kinds of monasteries existed in the same area, and the poor Poor Clares begged food from the rich Poor Clares. World events like the French Revolution, the Kulturkampf, the world wars of the last century, and communism nearly swept both away. What remains of Clare's movement today is variety. There is a bewildering abundance of differences among the many Poor Clares communities. The Poor Clares of Perpetual Adoration is only one of these communities; Mother Mary Francis's Poor Clares of the Colettine reform is another. When I asked Mother James the difference between them, she sighed at the task of explaining it and settled with, "They don't wear shoes." There is even variety among different monasteries within each community, but they all seem to be contemplative communities that practice a reasonable kind of poverty. No one in the Poor Clares of Perpetual Adoration monastery in downtown Cleveland winds up spending her life in bed because she doesn't eat enough— with fewer than twenty nuns in the house, I don't think they could afford the luxury of sacrificing flesh to faith. But they lead a poor life, patching their clothes over and over, eating more carrots and rice and bread than meat, and replacing broken old furniture with slightly sturdier old furniture. College students and welfare recipients expect a more sumptuous life.

But compared to the privations of even their recent past, Mother James and her nuns live well. I had asked Mother James several times about the early days of the downtown Cleveland monastery, but she didn't have much to say—she was so consumed by her duties as abbess that she didn't have the attention to spare. One day when I asked her yet again about the years before she was a postulant, she looked dazed and then suddenly relieved. "You can talk to Jimmy!" she said, doubtless happy to get me off her schedule for a few weeks. "He knows more about us than we do. He's been hanging around here since he was a little boy."

Jimmy turned out to be Anne's brother. On the day we were supposed to meet, Anne showed me to the parlor and I took my usual chair. After a while, Jimmy came in with a big envelope. He was dressed in dark pants and dark shoes with square brown glasses and had a look of seraphic sweetness to him. His hair was dark, too, while Anne's was white: I figured he was either her baby brother or had gotten all the family's youthful hair genes. He sat next to me, opened the envelope, and started to pull out what looked like letters and a diary, plus a fat, cheaply bound manuscript. I was greedy to start paging through them, but I turned my attention to him again. Anne had told me he was recently sick, and I wanted to find out how many of my questions he could bear. "Is today a good day to talk?"

"They're all good days to talk," he said cheerfully. "I can talk on any of them. Boy, can I talk!"

Both garrulous and charming, Jimmy was from one of Cleveland's old, blue-collar ethnic neighborhoods, a guy from a modest family who got a good education from the nuns and didn't use it to become a politician or businessman. Instead, Jimmy moved to New York to become a friar in what's called a third-order monastery—short form, it's a less regimented expression of Franciscan religious life than either the Poor Clares or Father Senan's Capuchins. He stayed there until 1960, when he decided that this wasn't the life for him. At first, he was ashamed of himself for leaving and ducked his head around his old Catholic-school friends back in Cleveland. By the time I talked to him, he felt that God had sent him to New York so that he could learn for himself what monastic life was like. He believed the experience allowed him to be a better friend, a stronger and more informed supporter, of his beloved Poor Clares.

Jimmy got hooked on the nuns while playing hooky. He sneaked away from school one day in the late 1940s, then realized there was really nothing for him to do: he had no money to spend and there were too many adults on the streets with suspicious eyes. As he ran past St. Paul, he darted in the front door and sat at the back of the church. The nuns were chanting the Divine Office and he was stunned by the rise and fall of their voices from behind the grates. He started coming to listen to the nuns legally, after school. "What I loved most was Tenebrae," he said, stopping to chant part of it himself, quavering along several octaves higher than his speaking voice, his hands breaking the syllables in the air. "I can't do it justice, honey. They sang it in three-part tone on the last three days of Holy Week at four in the afternoon, and it was just beautiful."

He became an altar boy at St. Paul and continued to hang around. The extern sisters started to ask little favors of him. Would he carry a heavy load up the stairs for them? Would he pick up something at the store? Then in 1950 when he was fourteen years old, Mother Agnes—the original abbess from Austria who brought the group to Cleveland in 1921—asked if he'd like to come inside and help them paint. This was *big*: in those days, the Church would excommunicate anyone who entered a cloister without permission and permission had to come from the bishop himself. But permission was granted, and Jimmy became the first man to walk among the nuns.

"I was thrilled!" he said, throwing up his arms when I asked him how he felt. Jimmy was one of those people with an animated lower lip and I watched it twist and tremble as he described his early days with the nuns. "I was thrilled half to death to work among them."

The nuns started Jimmy out in the garden, painting the rose trellises. He stood among the flowers and painted all day. He could hear the streetcars rattle past, out on the avenue, but that world was far away. He was surrounded by as much silence as sunshine, interrupted only by the day's rhythm of prayers, the Divine Office, floating out the windows of the church. Whenever he'd have to go to another part of the cloister, he'd ring a little bell to let the sisters know he was coming. Later, he worked on the walls, painting with a cluster of silent nuns, hearing only the slurp of brush in can, the rasp of paint on walls, maybe the occasional burble of soup cooking in the cloister's kitchen. Every hour, the nuns would put down their paintbrushes, fold their paint-splotched hands together and say a prayer. Every once in a while, one of them would leave and another would take her place. The new one would greet the others with, *"Adoremus in eternum"* (Let us adore him for eternity). The others would respond, *"Sanctissimum sacramentum"* (The most blessed sacrament).

Jimmy's face was dreamy as he told me all this. After he came back from the New York monastery, the Poor Clares hired him as their janitor. In 1992, they invited him to move into the monastery. He lived in one of the old abandoned rooms that used to hold postulants, where, he said, he found himself sinking more and more into prayer. He can't do much in the way of hard work anymore: he had a heart attack seven years ago, then was scalded when the monastery boiler blew up four years ago, then came down with colon cancer two years ago. After the heart attack, his own biological sisters teased him about all the attention he got from the nuns. "There were twenty-eight of them at the time, and my sisters said it was like I had twenty-eight mothers fussing over me." Jimmy rustled around in his chair, trying to find a way to resettle his legs more comfortably. He was wearing a blue-and-white plaid shirt, washed so many times that it shone a dull silver. As he moved, all its geometries changed. "I always had a wonderful feeling just knowing they were here."

"You've had quite a life." I was thinking how many people would find this a *terrible* life: growing old at the edge of a group of silent, celibate women who were also growing old. But

Jimmy's had been a life of serving—and now, just being around—something he found to be lovely and rare. When he opened the church door back in 1950 and heard the sounds of adoration, he had stumbled upon his own work of faith. I could understand how he stayed: sometimes I wondered if the reason I returned to St. Paul for mass every Sunday had less to do with my reaching toward God and more to do with the nuns themselves. They felt like a hearth of radiant love, even from my distance out in the pews. It made me feel good to know they were there, praying for all of us whether we had asked them to, whether we even believe such things matter. They were a constant, just as the stars are always there for an upward glance at wonder. Now that they knew I was there, a few of them had started to smile and wave at the end of mass before they filed out of their enclosure. My Sundays now demanded their presence—their presence from behind the grates, capped by cheesecake with the St. Paul regulars in the Guild Room and a hug from Sister Regina.

Jimmy seemed to guess my thoughts. "I often think how good God is, to let me share their life. They've always acted like Jesus sent me here to be their special friend."

As the years passed, Jimmy not only shoveled their snow and drove them to doctors and painted walls. He was also working with the late Sister Anne Marie to compile the group's history. That's what was stuffed in the fat envelope: different accounts of their history that no one has managed to complete. What looked like letters were Sister Anne Marie's efforts to distill the historical records and add her own memories. No one, as

I found out later, had gotten any further than the nuns' arrival in Cleveland in the 1920s, nearly a decade before they moved into the monastery attached to the shrine.

Jimmy was hoping I'd want to help him write a complete history of the order. He leaned forward to offer me an appealing tidbit. "These sisters really lived what they professed," he declared. "They were poor as church mice, right from the very beginning. When Mother Agnes first came to the States, they were looking all over the country, hoping to establish a monastery. They couldn't find a bishop to sponsor them. They went here and there, they even went to Milwaukee, but no luck. She told me they were so poor that their habits were falling apart. She went into a tailor's shop to see about getting some material to repair them. She heard the bells of the Angelus toll when she was there, and she fell to her knees. The tailor says to her, 'Sister, with prayers like that you can have the whole bolt!'"

"Is that story in these papers?" I asked.

He laughed. "No, that one's just in my head."

"But then Bishop Schrembs invited them to Cleveland and built them this monastery. They weren't as desperate then, were they?"

Jimmy looked shocked. "Honey, they were poorer! When I was a kid, I used to think the reason they hid themselves was because they didn't want anyone to see their ragged clothes. They had huge mortgage payments to make."

"The diocese didn't pay for the building?"

"They had huge mortgage payments," he said again. It seemed that the less said about the diocese the better. "I remember they used to have a novena once a month. They'd get out there in that courtyard and carry the statue of the baby Jesus around and pray they'd have enough money for the mortgage."

Memories of this kind of poverty—the kind you can't avoid—are powerful. My mother's memories of living poor as a girl and then poor again as a young wife during the Great Depression still guide her behavior. Even now that my parents lead a way-more-than-comfortable life, she can't abide waste. She blanches when someone pulls two paper towels off the roll instead of one. We sometimes find her poking at the top layer of the trash can after a big family meal, pulling out lightly used napkins and storing them under the sink so that she can wipe up spills with them later on. She tries to get through a meal without soiling her lips so that she doesn't get her own napkin dirty. Her children have always laughed at her, but even though she would never choose such poverty—and she certainly never romanticizes it as a simpler and better way to live—she could probably endure it better than any of us. I *do* romanticize poverty, which is probably one of the reasons I'm intrigued by the Poor Clares. I look around my house and sigh, convinced that my life would be so much easier if I didn't have all this stuff—even if I didn't have the means to buy all this stuff. Then I panic at the ominous ratio of bills to paychecks coming into the house, at the statistically probable three or four decades of life ahead of me and the burden of paying for them, at the sudden economic disasters that may wait for my little family, at the recognition of cosmic uncertainty forced by the end of my first marriage—then rush off to add a tiny Kosta Boda vase to the mantelpiece already crowded with an Inuit painting bought in a

Toronto gallery, the wrought-iron candlesticks, the Jenny Mendes and Daniel Postotnik ceramics, the antique clock in the shape of an antique clockmaker that my husband and I bought in Florence. What would it be like to step out of the cycle of wanting this cushion of objects and accoutrements and then hating them? Sometimes I look at my house and think of that poem about the man who receives a watch from his company and how the man must wind the watch and tend the watch and obey the watch, how in the end the watch really owns him. I think of my friend who returned from three years in the Peace Corps in Honduras, how she could hardly bear to go into the supermarket when she came home to Cleveland because she was so overwhelmed by the abundance of shampoo brands.

Two months after I spoke to Jimmy and carried away his papers, I was finally able to win an audience with Sister Mary Agnes. At ninety-three, she was the oldest nun in the group. She was the one I had seen a year ago when I sat in the Guild Room with Myron and Lynn, the one who had been in the monas- tery since 1935 (shortly after *Mother Agnes*—a different nun— founded the Cleveland community). When I arrived for our interview, she was already sitting in a chair next to her wheel- chair on the nuns' side of the parlor. She was much smaller than I had remembered, with dark, quick eyes, and she greeted me with a somber nod and watched intently as I pulled my chair up to the wall. We spoke for nearly two hours—a herculean effort on her part, since she had a headache as well as a dry mouth from all the pills she had to take—and for the longest time I thought I'd get nothing interesting from her. I asked— shouted, actually, since she was quite deaf—stupid questions like, "What's your strongest memory from the early years?" and she'd look at me skeptically and tell me to read the little history of the shrine that had been printed on one of the mass bulletins. I brought out a monograph that had been published in the 1980s to celebrate St. Paul's fiftieth anniversary as a Catholic church, hoping that the pictures in it would shift the tide of her memories, but she looked through it and put her small, crooked fingers on face after face. "Dead. Dead. This one dead too," she said quietly. Then somehow we hit upon the subject of poverty. All of a sudden, her memories began to animate her.

"I remember that my first Christmas here I was very sad." She sounded slightly aggrieved still. "We were so very poor. And when I came down to breakfast that morning, we had hard bread with coffee, same as every other morning. When I saw that it just struck my heart, because it was Christmas and we were having the same bread we had every morning."

"Every morning?" I said, trying to keep her talking.

"What?"

"Every morning!"

"Yes, every morning. Since Vatican Two, it's all different. Now they can have toast or cereal or fruit in the morning."

I had to smile at the image that popped into my head: that of a roomful of cardinals in Rome debating the relative poverty of cereal or toast, whole wheat or rye. These seemed like the pettiest of details, especially ludicrous if they were being decided by a group of men who lived in what I considered palatial luxury. But Mother James always defended their attention to these details—in fact, she often writes to Rome to ask for guidance—explaining that the Poor Clares must guard against any distractions from their prayer life. The shopping for an expanded selection of things, the attachment that can develop for a particularly appealing thing, even the time taken to choose between one thing and another: all these are troublesome interruptions to contemplation. She had told me about their problem with nightgowns. After Vatican II, nuns were allowed to abandon their traditional going-to-bed cotton habit and nighttime veil. The Poor Clares might have continued this tradition, but suddenly those habits weren't even available from the religious supply stores. So they decided to use simple white gowns. However, the white gowns quickly morphed into pink or polka-dotted gowns, and the community decided this was too much attention to something that doesn't matter. The nightgowns are now a somber, simple black, all in the same style.

And just as the Poor Clares community as a whole struggles to wean itself from the allures of plenitude, individual nuns struggle to accommodate the community's decisions. "How did you manage to accept the plain bread on that Christmas morning?" I asked Sister Agnes, my voice so loud that I was afraid it carried all the way into the church.

She shrugged. "Our superior came from a wealthy family, and I was from a poor family. Who am I, that I couldn't take it? I ate the hard bread."

During those pre–Vatican II days, the nuns were divided into three groups: the choir sisters, who kept up the adoration; the lay sisters, who did the cooking, cleaning, and laundry; and the extern sisters, who were the monastery's liaisons to the outside world. Sister Agnes was always an extern sister. During the lean years of the 1930s and 1940s, she told me that their abbess used to walk around with a stack of bills the size of a dictionary; she used to exhort the nuns, "Pray! Pray that we can pay off our debts!" The building alone cost $1.5 million and it took the nuns forty years to pay it off. As an extern, Sister Agnes didn't spend her hours behind the grates praying for the community's solvency. She was on the outside, scrambling for food. As she told her stories—and they came quickly now—it was like listening to a runner talking about races won.

"We extern sisters used to go out to the farms and work for food." She darted glances at me, then looked at her hands. "Sometimes people weren't honest. I remember once a good woman took us out to a farm. We worked under the hot sun and weeded the farmer's peppers and his beans. When we were finished, we asked if we could take a little of the produce back to the other sisters. He told us he had nothing to spare."

Then, Sister Agnes decided not to bother with the farmers anymore. She asked one of the lay people to drive her to Cleveland's wholesale food terminal, where produce from around the country rolled into town before dawn and area grocers did their shopping before most of their customers were out of bed. She went from one purveyor to another to beg food for the nuns. For thirty years, she kept fresh fruit and vegetables in the cloister kitchen by begging.

I asked her if begging was difficult. Her sharp old eyes stopped darting around and she smiled. She had deep dimples, lovely olive skin, elegantly arched nares—Gothic arches, I thought. There again, not only Clare's commitment to poverty but also her beauty. "I loved doing it," she exclaimed. "We were poor, we had nothing, and it was a joy to ask people to give. And they had joy by giving. I got to know these people so well that they'd have baskets of food waiting for me. They were so generous. Even the Jewish people were generous with us."

She peered at me as if waiting for a dubious reaction, then went on. "I have a Jewish friend with a bakery and every Christmas Eve he comes down with a load of fresh rolls. He brings his wife and children. His son throws his arms around me like I'm a member of the family. This has been going on for fifty years. Before him, his father did it."

She had many other stories of their poverty: after all, she was the workhorse who took what little they had and stretched it until it was just enough. For instance, there was the story of the paint. When the monastery was built, there hadn't been enough money to paint the interior walls. Sister Agnes thought that people who came to the parlors shouldn't have to look at raw plaster, so she asked Mother Agnes for paint. There was no money for paint, but then a few parishioners donated some. As she started to work on the rooms, Sister Agnes realized that the donated paint would not be enough: she had only an inch left in the bottom of the final bucket, but still had a whole second coat to put on the last parlor. Mother Agnes told her there would be no more paint and that she'd have to make this little bit last. And Sister Agnes did: she prayed over that last bucket, prayed that God would allow it to be enough. As in the parable of the loaves and the fishes, that last inch of paint continued to fill her brush and brighten the walls. Sister Agnes told me that she finished the last parlor and still had paint to spare.

She looked at me triumphantly, then pressed her hand to her temple: the story of the paint had only temporarily distracted her from her headache. I thanked her for her time and started to gather my things. She watched me close my notebook, then narrowed her eyes.

"How much are you charging for this?"

I didn't understand what she was asking. Maybe she thought I was working on the brochure that I had promised to write for Mother James. "Today, I was interviewing you for the book I'm writing," I assured her. "I'm also going to write some vocation literature for Mother James, but I'm not charging her for that."

"But what are you charging for this book?"

Poverty was a habit. Sister Agnes was still wary that some financial misstep might threaten the community; she was still thinking of the beans that the farmer withheld, still watching their pennies. Again I was reminded of my mother, who asks me how much my supermarket is charging for eggs and is shocked when I don't know.

"I'm not charging anything for the book," I told her. "It's just something I want to do. You've already given me your time."

"It's always best to ask," she said fretfully. She looked around the room that she had brightened so many years ago with her last inch of paint. "Things are so expensive these days. We have to have fresh flowers in front of the Blessed Sacrament and candles, at least six but it's better with twelve. That's canon law. It's very difficult."

She took my hand in hers and kissed it. "I love you," she said. Usually, the people who say that get an automatic "I love you" back, but it didn't seem right: she was loving me as a fellow creature made in the image of God, and my love is confined to a much tinier slice of humanity. I asked if I could help her into her wheelchair, but she shook her head and waited until I left the room. I stood just outside the door as she gripped the bars of the dividing wall between her world and mine and resettled herself, trying to decide whether the sounds I heard signaled distress or determination.

With the exception of Sister Regina, all the Poor Clares I had met so far were well over the age of sixty. Meeting Sister Agnes had tipped the age scale for me: I had stopped thinking of the group of nuns as "young old" and worried that they were sliding inexorably toward "old old." The next time I met with Mother James, I asked what had happened to the woman from Arizona who had expressed interest in joining the community. I half expected her to tell me that she had lost interest or that they had found out about something that disqualified her. "Oh, Joanna—she's already been here for a month," Mother James said casually. "She's a real firecracker."

"Can I talk to her?"

"Oh, no! She's got enough to handle."

I was greedy for information. "Is she your age or my age or younger? What did she do before she came here?"

"She's in her early thirties. And she's half Irish and half Colombian, I think." She waved away further questions. "We also have another new postulant. You know Valerie, don't you?"

I did know Valerie, although only by sight. She was a young woman—not much older than my daughter, I guessed— who had worked for the nuns over the past year. I had passed her several times on my way to the parlor; she was often head-ing in the opposite direction with an armload of mops or a pile of boxes. And now she was on the inside!

I thought that the appearance of these new women was a remarkable development. There had been very few new postulants in the last decade: one had arrived five years ago, the other nine years ago. Was it possible that a tiny rebirth was beginning in the Poor Clares' cloister? Could this presage the dawning of a new interest in adoration that would fill the monastery with fresh prayers? This was the thought that dazzled me all the way home. I hadn't yet considered how hard it would be for the long-established Poor Clares to absorb these young women into their terribly secluded intimacy. And I hadn't considered how hard it would be for these new women to adjust to a lifestyle centered around the assumed yet unseen presence of God—to not only give up lavender peignoirs at night and French toast in the morning, but all the intangible pleasures of the world outside.

8

My first foray into extended prayer was painful—quite literally filled with small but nettlesome pains. St. Paul's kneelers were covered in a brown linoleum-like material patterned to look like marble and they truly *felt* like marble to my finicky left knee, injured months earlier when I wore shoes with heels that were too high. I couldn't find much comfort sitting, either, as the pews are plain hard wood with emphatically erect backs and not enough sitting area from knee to butt—it seems the Victorians who built the church had even stubbier legs than I. And I wasn't much more comfortable when I stood, since my knee and back twinged from the kneeling and the sitting. The problem was that I had committed myself to twelve hours of this—*an entire night of prayer*—and probably the last time I stayed up all night had been twenty-two years earlier, when I was giving birth to my daughter. When you're in the middle of labor, you can't just decide you've had your quota of discomfort and go home. However, discomfort can easily trump fainthearted faith. I could already hear myself telling myself that this was a silly gesture, that I didn't belong with this group of disconcertingly fervent believers, and that I had already seen enough in the first hour to know what the whole night would be like. Then I forestalled all that potential rationalizing with a question: You can't stick this out for one night? Not even one night?

So this, then, was my recurring prayer throughout the vigil: Please, God, help me stay the night. And here was my ancillary prayer: Please, God, don't let me fall asleep and make a spectacle of myself. The woman at the end of my pew must not have said that particular prayer. She fell asleep kneeling with her head bent over an arm resting on the back of the next pew and had to flail noisily to keep herself from crashing to the floor. It was the only eventful moment in a half-hour stretch of silent prayer shortly after midnight. Everyone else in the church startled, looked her way, then continued their own meditations with carefully squared shoulders.

Only a few weeks earlier, I had met with two sisters who hold leading positions in the diocese to talk about the Poor Clares of Perpetual Adoration and nuns in general. Sister Marietta Starrie and Sister Mary Rose Kocab are part of the great wave of modern nuns who wear business suits and blue jeans, live in scattered apartments instead of convents, are involved in a wide range of nontraditional ministries, and have generally abandoned what many refer to as the medieval trappings of religion. I had read a book that claimed that the changes initiated by Vatican II had raged out of control and were responsible for the vast reductions in the ranks of the religious, and I wondered what they would think of this theory.

I also wanted to know what they thought of the Poor Clares themselves, who not only clung to many of these medieval trappings but also led a life far removed from the impassioned activism of modern nuns.

But these two weren't about to get sucked into a debate about the merits of modern versus traditional religious life. Sister Marietta wrinkled her nose when I mentioned this particular book, then recommended another that she thought presented changes in the sisterhood with greater balance. "We're all needed," Sister Mary Rose said when I asked them if they thought the Poor Clares were wasting their lives behind the grates. "Religious life is a mystery. None of us has a complete vision of what God is calling us to do today. We're always wrestling with it."

"I have to visit the Colettine Poor Clares from time to time," Sister Marietta said. "I often leave feeling envious that they have all that time for contemplation and that I don't. But then, I have to remind myself that that's not where God is calling me."

Sister Mary Rose turned to her. "I might have gone away from them thinking about what my life is missing. Maybe God *is* calling you to think about contemplation."

The two of them bracketed me in age—I guessed that the small, silver-haired Marietta was about ten years older and the huskier, red-haired Mary Rose was about ten years younger—and their back-and-forth had the patina of an ongoing discussion. As my meeting with them went on, it became clear that religious life is, even for them, a moving target, that they are always searching for the hairpin twists and turns in their spiritual path. Everything, even Sister Marietta's pang upon leaving the Colettine Poor Clares, can be seized as a breadcrumb dropped by God in the cosmic forest. They sounded sort of New Age at times, but not so much that it got on my nerves. At least neither said they wanted to "share" with me, an utterance that always makes me want to stretch my claws and say, "You can *share* your M&Ms with me but please just *tell* me your thoughts." They were earnest women, struggling to apply the two-thousand-year-old teachings of their Church to the world as it is now, to combine these teachings with other sacred and secular traditions to illuminate lives of meaning.

Some of the trappings of Catholicism for which I was still nursing a nostalgic fondness—the habits, for instance—were no longer an issue for these women. When I asked them if they missed the old style of dress, they looked politely aghast. I had to acknowledge, inwardly, that it was pretty self-indulgent of me to expect today's religious women to suffer the wimple so that I could be reminded of the lovely nuns of my childhood. Or maybe, I thought later, maybe my longing for their traditional dress wasn't connected to my childhood: maybe I just wanted to see visible declarations of faith so that I didn't worry that I was working my way back to something that was about to disappear. Ash Wednesday seems to be about the only time that Catholics stand out in the ordinary sprawl of life, walking down the street and eating at cafes and talking on their cell phones with their soot-blackened foreheads. In the last few years, I've discovered a pleasure in Ash Wednesday that used to be reserved for Halloween. I have the same kind of question for everyone on that day—"What are you going to be?"—that I used to ask before Halloween. In the case of Ash Wednesday, I can see their answer written over their eyes.

In any case, these two contemporary nuns had moved on and were part of the Church's continuing evolution. Sister Mary Rose worked with young people throughout the diocese who have a leaning toward religious life, some of whom were creating informal communities that combined contemplation, evangelism, and activism. She told me that most of the sisters from older orders like her own, the Sisters of the Incarnate Word, were activists within corporate structures. They sat on boards of foundations, hospitals, and universities, pushing for structural change and urging the organizations to use their investments to help the poor. The religious fledglings were street-level activists, serving their God by joining hands with the poor.

So the great division that I had imagined between traditional and contemporary nuns wasn't so great after all; like all lines drawn in the sand, it moved with the tides. Sister Mary Rose had recently spent some time at her order's monastery in France, where the nuns work with the sick and elderly and also maintain perpetual adoration. "I was so refreshed and soothed by my stay there," she said, "and then I thought, 'Back to the real world.' But I started to wonder if that environment wasn't more real than all the trappings we put on our life here. Sometimes I wonder if we've tried too hard to make ourselves relevant. We blend into our culture and our times so much that we've lost the mystique, the prophetic edge that I believe religious life has to have."

"I've wondered about that," I told her. "You two run around to meetings all day and go home to an empty apartment at night and"—I glanced at their business cards—"you have e-mail."

"I have two e-mail addresses!" Sister Mary Rose said. "Maybe that's my problem."

"So how are the two of you different from other women who do good work and pray and don't have sexual relations?"

"The difference is that the primary relationship in my life is with God," she said slowly, her blue eyes light-infused and earnest. "That's what sustains me."

But this may not be enough to attract new vocations. In the Cleveland area there are slightly more women joining the traditional orders than those with navy suits and e-mail. Sister Mary Rose said that not all of these stay, though. She believes that some of the young people who are attracted to the more traditional orders never had much structure growing up and are yearning for clear guidelines to faith. "But you don't join religious life for the structure," she added. "You join a religious order to have a deep, passionate, intimate relationship with God. Whatever lifestyle helps you have that relationship, that's the one you should have. Some people get fascinated with the mystique of the rituals and the habits, but this fascination won't sustain you."

I found all this intriguing. Certainly, one of the things that drew me to my Poor Clares was their mystique: the rustle of their robes as I followed them through the dusty outer rooms of their monastery, their daylong silence, their obscurity behind the grates, their twenty-four-hour cycle of prayer, their fairly recent history of bodily mortification and other practices that seem nearly psychotic when viewed through modern eyes. A few of the Poor Clares had mentioned these practices but had been unwilling to talk about them. Finally, I met one of the older nuns who was able to discuss them without squeamishness. I was running late when I went to interview Sister Mary Anselm. As I took my seat, I saw bright metal grillwork behind her and thought, idiotically, "Shopping cart?" It was one of those walkers equipped with a metal basket. However difficult it was for her to reach this room, she was sitting in one of the chairs with an erect posture and queenly mien, as if her dark veil were a royal robe. I noticed how hers was another lovely face: she looked like Grace Kelly playing the role of an elderly nun. When Sister Anselm saw me, though, she smiled as eagerly as a child on her way to a picnic. This impression of youthfulness persisted in the oh-gosh inflections of her voice—she sounded a little like Judy Garland in *The Wizard of Oz*—even though she was eighty years old. She wore no glasses, but I could see a pink eyeglasses case in the basket of her walker. Vanity, I wondered, or does she just not need them all the time?

"I didn't want to do this when Mother first asked," she said as I took my seat, handing me an index card imprinted with her address, date of birth, the date she joined the Poor Clares and the date she made her solemn vows. "I figured you were interviewing the whole group and that I'd just creep away after you got going. When I heard that you wanted to meet us one-on-one, I really didn't want to come. I asked Father if I should meet with you and he said, 'God uses strange tools.' "

"Am I a strange tool?"

She laughed. "There's another expression: 'God writes straight with crooked lines.' Have you heard that one, Sister?"

I put down my pen and wondered if she thought I was someone else.

"Oh, did you hear me call you Sister?" She laughed again. "I'm so used to living with nuns and saying, 'Sister this' and 'Sister that.' I can't help myself."

She called me Sister for the next two hours.

Sister Anselm was another of the Poor Clares who knew from an early age that she wanted to be a contemplative nun. For a while, though, she drifted away from God: she left her family farm for Chicago, had a job working as a secretary for a cargo plane manufacturer, had many dates and friends, and the desire to become a nun was only a spark at the edge of her life. Then she changed jobs. Since there was a shrine nearby, she started going to daily mass, and the desire to become a nun was rekindled. She prepared to enter a convent, but her older sister told her that she needed to take in their ailing mother, so she found a new apartment with room for her mother. They were happy together. She doted on her mother, combing her hair, sewing her clothes; she said she would have been happy tending her until her last breath. However, her ecclesiastical clock was ticking: she was twenty-nine years old and the convents wouldn't take her past the age of thirty. She thought this was her last chance to go with God, so she made the wrenching decision to leave her mother with her sister.

Her mother lived another four years and then died in a nursing home. "I had to be selfish then," Sister Anselm said. "I had to follow my vocation. And my mother never said a thing against it."

She looked at the floor as she finished this story, looking still like a child only this time like one about to be chastised. She brightened when I asked if the Poor Clares monastery was all that she'd hoped it would be. "Yes, but no one ever smiled, and that's not my disposition," she said, looking radiant again. "I smile all the time. When I went to the community room that first night, they all hugged me and told me they hoped I had the perseverance. It would have been chilling if it weren't for Jesus, but he was the warmth."

"They don't seem so serious now," I said.

"It's not like that anymore." She beamed again and the white band encircling her face puckered around her eyes. "They all smile except Mother. She's very good and has great spiritual wisdom, but I have to tell her to smile all the time."

I asked her if things had changed much from those early days. She shrugged. "The discipline is different," she said. "We used to have to discipline ourselves three times each week."

"What do you mean, discipline?" I imagined the nuns pacing back and forth in their tiny bedrooms, scolding themselves.

She pantomimed it for me, gripping an imaginary whip with two hands and swinging it over one shoulder, then the other. "You had to turn off the lights and discipline yourself and say the Misere."

"You hit yourselves?"

She nodded again. At first, I felt a hint of youthful naughtiness about her. I was reminded of the way the older kids at Gold Lake Y camp loved to tell new kids lurid stories about murderous trail guides whenever we went on our weekly midnight hike. Then I realized that this was a woman who didn't particularly care what I thought; beneath all the smiles, she was a strong personality with fierce convictions and she felt no compunction to gloss over the things that might make me or anyone else blanch. "At night, we'd have to get a basin of water and wash ourselves sitting on the floor. I often ate on the floor," she continued. "These were penances, and I'd do all of them that I could."

"What else?"

"Sometimes I'd attend the entire mass with a rope around my neck."

I suppose that I unsuccessfully suppressed a grimace, since I saw that Sister Anselm was looking greatly amused. Still, I had known that some orders practiced such penances. In fact, I had already been reading about them in a fascinating book called *I Leap Over the Wall*. The book was written by Monica Baldwin, a former nun who left the strictly enclosed world of a centuries-old British convent in 1941, after living there for nearly thirty years. Baldwin was Rip van Winkle times two: not only was the secular world different from the world of the convent, but it was also vastly different from the prim, mannered, leisurely world that had disappeared over the course of the First World War. The changes were evident even before she left the convent, when her sister arrived to take her back to London

and handed her a set of clothes suitable for the world outside
the convent walls:

> *The crescendo of shocks which awaited me began abruptly*
> *with my first introduction to up-to-date underwear. Frankly,*
> *I was appalled. The garments to which I was accustomed had*
> *been contrived by thorough-going ascetics in the fourteenth*
> *century, who considered that a nice, thick, long-sleeved "shift"*
> *of rough, scratchy serge was the right thing to wear next to*
> *your skin . . . Stays, shoulder-strapped and severely boned,*
> *concealed one's outline; over them, two long serge petticoats*
> *were lashed securely around one's waist. Last came the ample*
> *habit-coat of heavy cloth, topped by a linen rochet and a*
> *stiffly starched barbette of cambric, folded into a score of tiny*
> *tucks and pleats at the neck. So when my sister handed me a*
> *wisp of gossamer, about the size and substance of a spider's*
> *web, I was shocked. I examined the garment, remembering*
> *1914. In those days a "nice" girl "started" with long wooly*
> *combinations, neck-high and elbow-sleeved, decorated with a*
> *neat set of pearl buttons down the front . . .*

Baldwin braved reentry into the madcap, make-do years of England during World War II. She decided that it was actually a
propitious time for a cloistered nun to hurl herself outside since
society was in such tremendous flux. But she didn't write the
book to catalogue her adventures in the secular world, although
they were remarkable. She wrote the book because so many
people on the outside recoiled when she told them she'd been

in a convent, and she wanted to explain what goes on inside and why. She undertook this explanation with the greatest respect for those who are called to the contemplative life—she concedes that it took her far too long to realize she was not one of them—as well as a bracing intellectualism, as she pulled together much that had been written about contemplatives during the preceding centuries.

Baldwin explains that convent life and rules of behavior were devised so that as little as possible distracted the nuns from their contemplation of God. Even such small details as the way they walked was predetermined: they should keep their hands clasped at the waist, take tiny steps, and keep their eyes down at all times. Even the swinging of the arms implied a breach, an extravagance of being. In her day, nuns weren't even allowed to see newspapers, and she spent all of the First World War in near-total oblivion of what was going on outside. This alienation is less severe for today's Poor Clares, but much is still proscribed: no television, no radio, no frequent visits, nothing to pull their attention far from God. All this only makes sense given a certain understanding of the contemplative's goal. "God, lovelier than any dream, is pure Spirit," Baldwin writes. "Therefore, if contact is to be established, the counter-attraction of the senses must be overcome. You can't be completely wrapped up in God (and he is a jealous lover), unless you are unwrapped-up in what this world has to offer you. In convents, this process of unwrapping is effected by a system of remorseless separation from everything that is not God."

If her new secular acquaintances found statements like this dauntingly absurd—and some did—they had far greater problems when she tried to explain penances to them. Baldwin writes that one of the things that astounded her the most when she left the convent was the modern world's fixation on food. In the convent, the nuns ate only enough to sustain themselves for their intended work. More than that was considered gluttony. In addition, the nuns were supposed to "mortify" their palate at least once during every meal—to eat something they didn't like or pass up something they fancied. When her friends pressed for an example, Baldwin offered the story of a nun who transferred pieces of fat and gristle from the communal plate of scraps to her own—and ate them. After a horrified silence, one of her worldly, well-manicured friends said, "Darling, of course it may be most frightfully holy and all that to go about devouring garbage, but to me it seems simply too, too revolting. And how it can possibly benefit anyone is quite beyond me."

I have the feeling that Baldwin's anecdote may have been inspired by the same yearn to shock the spiritually timorous that I sensed in Sister Anselm, and it had the intended effect. On me, as well: I also find the idea of eating someone else's discarded gristle loathsome. Still, I am intrigued by Baldwin's explanation for this and other penances: the discipline with whips, the haircloths, the studded metal bracelets, wooden crosses with exposed nails, and chain girdles that were worn to inflict pain. In her view, such voluntary practices weren't lunacy but a kind of heroism.

> *Mortification [was] the painful, monotonous job of putting to death one's "natural inclinations" so that the "supernatural" life of grace might take complete possession of one's soul . . . It is interesting to note that the extraordinary penances of the saints were not so much the outcome of a desire for their own sanctification as a tremendous urge to help and save and if possible atone for the sins and sufferings of the world which has very largely lost the true idea of God. The [contemplative] life itself—hard, silent, rigorous, austere—is packed with opportunities for self-denial. And yet, for many souls, even that does not seem to be enough.*

Within a decade or two, Baldwin's convent was probably shaken by the religious upheaval inspired by Vatican II. Just as life in the Poor Clares monastery changed, it is likely that much of what Baldwin says about her convent is outdated—*except* for the spiritual underpinning. The foundation remains the same, but what springs from it seems to be far less severe these days. When I asked Sister Anselm why the penances have changed but other things haven't—why priests still can't marry and women can't be ordained—she made a dismissive gesture. "Oh, these penances weren't essentials," she said. "It wasn't essential that I eat on the floor. What really matters is that we love God and love our neighbor." So the Poor Clares have stripped away some of the more rigorous measures that burned a pathway to God. What's left is the denial of nearly all of the pleasures the rest of us take for granted. Their life still only makes sense if you believe, as Baldwin writes, that "God is not just some vague, remote, spiritual ideal, but a living Person.

[Believers] therefore become possessed by a kind of burning hunger and thirst for God which only he himself can satisfy . . . it is possible for the veil to be lifted and for the human soul to enter into what is, literally, a conscious, experimental contact with God. And those who have experienced this contact declare unanimously that it can only be described as a foretaste of the bliss of heaven."

Mother James had told me this months before: that nothing the Poor Clares do makes sense without this belief. On the other hand, Sister Marietta, Sister Mary Rose, and other noncontemplative nuns pursue a range of activities that make sense whether or not one even believes in God. I pointed this out to them, and they readily agreed. "Their lifestyle is radical," Sister Mary Rose said. "It's kind of like 'raw God.' "

Then she told me about a retreat she made several years ago at a monastery run by Trappists, contemplative monks who are not quite as strictly traditional or secluded as the Poor Clares of Perpetual Adoration. She decided she would follow their routine and get up in the middle of the night to join them in prayer. "I was overcome," Sister Mary Rose said, then reached up to cover her eyes. When she removed her hands, the tears kept flowing and she wiped them on the cuff of her navy suit. "I am again, just talking about them. I was so moved to know that throughout the world, there is always this presence that is praying. That I was there with this motley group of men who stay up all night to hold the world in prayer."

"I'm going to be doing something like that, too." I was

also moved by the thought of someone praying day and night, and I felt my own vaporous flush of tears. I don't know how to explain this, except that it comforts me to know that the Trappists and the Poor Clares and contemplatives from other traditions maintain this steady, hidden stream of prayer. It comforts me so deeply that it's unsettling. "The Poor Clares are having a public all-night prayer vigil—their first since the 1940s," I continued. "I decided I'm going to try to stay the night, all the way to mass at dawn." That declaration marked my formal commitment. I had been telling my friends I'd do this for the last couple of weeks, but I hadn't put my name on the vigil list posted in the church lobby or told Sister Regina. I didn't want to disappoint her by deciding at the foot of my driveway that dinner with friends or just a night at home with my husband and the dogs and all our ordinary pleasures might seem overwhelmingly sweet when compared to a night in church. But I felt I couldn't renege if I told Sister Mary Rose of my intentions. After all, she might come herself and wonder where I was.

So there I was two weeks later, pulling into the church parking lot just before nine o'clock. I was a little nervous on the dark sidewalk leading to the church, especially since there was a knot of unfamiliar men smoking around one of the spindly young trees near the street. It turned out that these men were stationed there for my protection; they waved me toward the light streaming from the church doors. Inside, about sixty people were scattered around the pews. Sister Regina was kneeling in the last row. There was the kind of muffled racket that comes from a lot of people trying to be quiet. Three enormous standing fans—truly, they had blades that could fly a small plane from Cleveland to Detroit—rotated from side to side, blasting periodic hot air my way and making the hundreds of tiny flames in red glass candle holders flicker. I could hear the men laughing outside and some people talking in only slightly hushed voices in the Guild Room. I looked back and saw Sister Regina frown and cock her head toward the voices. I didn't recognize any of the people around me and they were all praying silently. Then I noticed a printed program and a prayer book on the seat next to me. I saw that each hour had been divided into a routine of songs, readings from the book—a sweet-smelling missal printed in the 1950s called "The Eucharistic Vigil"—then silent prayer. I looked at my watch and saw that it was almost time for another hourly cycle. Then a group of people walked into the church. A man a few pews ahead of me picked up a guitar, a woman next to him held a small, handheld microphone to her lips, and we began.

I made it through the first hour of songs, prayers, and silence handily enough, then went out to get a cup of coffee in the Guild Room. Someone had made a very nice batch of banana bread, and I took a slice. I listened to the chatter of people standing by the coffeepot. A cherub-faced young blonde introduced herself as Kim and asked which parish I was from and seemed surprised when I said none. Lynn came into the room and got into conversation with an old man whose skin was so thin and tight to the bone it looked as if it had been painted on. "I've asked to join over and over," she said in response to something the old man had said. "They've turned me down every time." I wondered if she was talking about the Poor Clares: Along with Joanna and Valerie, had she also asked them to accept her as a postulant?

The second hour was harder because it was so much like the first. I yawned, I shifted my body every few minutes to keep parts of it from falling asleep, I paid attention to the mild idiosyncracies of the people around me. While the rest of us droned, there was a woman a few pews back who enunciated the words of each prayer as if speaking to someone hard of hearing. There were several people with rosaries, and I watched them finger their prayers as deftly as others tally sums on an abacus. One man conducted an elaborate routine during silent prayer. He backed down the aisle, stopping at each pew, where he made the sign of the cross about twenty times in the air in front of his face, then got down on both knees, then rose to back up again. But none of this seemed remarkable to me. It was only remarkable that I was there and that I felt nothing. I remembered talking to Sister Mary Rose about her night of prayer with the Trappists; I remembered how her story had moved me to tears. "I too am helping to hold the world in prayer," I told myself, hoping to break through my unrelenting shell. Still, I felt nothing, no rush of conviction, no overwhelming sense of being with God.

I knew that it was during a night like this that God lassoed Sister Mary Joseph. She was one of the newest and youngest of the Poor Clares. At the time of my all-night prayer vigil, she had yet to take her final vows. It was her lovely soprano voice that was now leading the others behind the grates at mass every week, even though she had never done any formal singing before she joined the cloister. I met her the week before the vigil, and she had explained that there was a distinct Before and After to her life. Before: she was a registered nurse who worked in labor and delivery, had tons of friends, hoped to marry, went to baseball and football games and could be heard shouting at the teams from the opposite side of the stadium, thought about buying a Harley, went skydiving. Then things got a little slow at work. She had time to fill, and when her church asked its younger members to sign up for a weekly hour of adoration, she agreed. But she blew through her first hour; she was too busy Christmas shopping, so her father took her hour. She blew through her second hour, too. She finally made it to her third hour, but didn't quite know what to do with herself. She sat there and prayed the Rosary. She told me the whole point was to keep God company, to answer the question Jesus is said to have asked two millennia past: Can you not sit with me for just one hour?

Then the going became a habit. This was still Before, though, and becoming a nun was the furthest thing from her mind. She was planning to get involved with a new maternity center for single teenagers, she was planning all sorts of things, and then she toppled suddenly into After. She was sitting in her bedroom at home reading about St. Bridget, who was supposedly told by God that if she would pray for a year she would never suffer the pains of purgatory. Sister Joseph was struck by God's eagerness for connection, how he would offer people these new elaborations on faith just to pull them closer to him. "I just fell in love," Sister Joseph said, her teeth making a pearly scalloped edge against her rough lower lip. "I don't know how else to describe it." As with any infatuation, she wanted more contact with her beloved. She went to daily mass for the next four months. One day, she was driving past a church and said out loud, "I love you so much I wish I could marry you." Then she struck herself on the forehead: *Bride of Christ!* A few days later, her letter carrier slipped a neighbor's copy of a Catholic magazine under her door by mistake. Clare of Assisi, celebrating her eight-hundredth birthday, was the cover girl.

One of the reasons I had come to the vigil was curiosity: I had wondered if a night in the shrine would trip the wires of my own version of Before and After. As I followed along with the vigil routine and clung to my place in the pew for the next few hours, I monitored the impact of the prayers, the songs, the candles, the people bowed and weary, the unblinking white eye of the host. I waited to see if the tendrils of faith would tickle my ankles.

Several of my friends had been teasing me about this prayer vigil. One told me she half expected me to call one day and tell her I'd decided to join the monastery. No danger of that, I replied: these Poor Clares won't take women with children and a husband, not even women with no children and a recent ex-husband just in case there is the possibility of reconciliation. But even I wondered where all this might lead. Over the past year and a half, I'd find myself drifting perilously close to belief, then panic. "Oh, no," I'd think, "then I'll have to be . . ." But be what? Good? I'm already good in a simple, text-book kind of way: I hardly ever lie, and I don't cheat, steal, dis-honor my parents, screw around, or murder. Was the peril of belief giving up my freedom to be bad? Was it that I'd be com-pelled toward some more active state of goodness that I don't even understand? Or was it that the world is so full of stupid, dreadfully earnest believers of one kind or another, people who would never question their faith or anything else, and I'm too vain to want to be lumped in with them?

Even if there was some sort of After for me—some sort of life in faith—I knew I didn't want to be the kind of person who goes around trying to urge others to join me. I had already done enough proselytizing when I was a member of a Maoist group during and after college, and I swore I'd never do it again. My attraction to this group had started in much the same way as my disaffection with the faith of my childhood. I was sitting in a college biology class, and the teacher said something about the connection between the corporate drive for profits and pollu-tion. All of a sudden, all the things I found appalling in our society were caught up in the wheels of capitalism: this seemed to be the neat, pure explanation for all evils. When I saw my col-lege roommate looking at an SDS leaflet about a campus meet-ing, I said, "Sign me up for everything!" She didn't, but I transferred in a year to another college that swarmed with such groups. The hallway to the student cafeteria was jammed with student-activism peddlers; it was a smorgasbord of thrilling radical ideas. I became involved with one of these groups, although not because I had carefully analyzed what each had to say. There was a skinny, sweet, Harley-riding boy from New

York—I fell in love with him and later married him—who was attracted to this group, for reasons that I think were similarly apolitical.

Many years later, people are shocked to hear that placid, suburban I was a Maoist at one time—that the FBI used to visit the places where my husband worked and get him fired, that I was arrested several times in demonstrations, that we used to get the occasional death-threat call in the middle of the night. People think this must have been an exhilarating desperado life, but it was not: after only a few years of it, my days were filled with either ennui or dread. The early years *were* exciting: creeping across a railroad trestle with members of the Black Panther Party to plot an escape should the police attack their office; talking all night with the disaffected city youth who filled our shabby downtown office; shucking college for a more "rel-evant" antiestablishment lifestyle. But as the group went national and began to focus on clarifying its political beliefs, I started to hate the path I had chosen. My days were consumed by factory jobs in which I was supposed to convince my coworkers of the need for revolution, but they were far more interested in Tupperware parties or saving for their vacations in Bermuda. My nights were consumed by meetings that went on for hours trying to hammer down the correct political line and make sure that everyone was hammered into agreement with it. My boredom was replaced by dread every time I had to go out and sell this political line to strangers—in the form of our little newspaper—on street corners, outside factory gates, and in unemployment offices. I made the pitch with difficulty, head down and words tumbled together. Many people were hostile; some were just wryly amused. There were probably a number of people who couldn't even understand what I was saying. One man made this abundantly clear. As I blurted out my plea that he buy a *copy* of our newspaper, he stopped and regarded me with kindly confusion. "Did you say something about *cowboys*?" he asked.

In my year and a half of going to mass, there was one moment that always thrilled me. It was when the nuns and whole congregation sang this line somewhere in the middle of the service: "Blessed is he who comes in the name of the Lord!" I loved the idea that someone could manage to be so mindful of the divine that they brought it with them wherever they went— that they were sort of a walking manifestation of God. I imagined that the people who carried this sense of the divine shone with it, could help heal withered hopes and wounded hearts. Unlike my former conversion to Maoist thought, I didn't think I'd have to make speeches or hector people with slogans if I were one of those coming in the name of the Lord. I'd have to fill up with grace, with the radiance of belief. But how did people do that?

As we approached two o'clock, I was amazed that I had made it that far. Still, I felt no special tug from the divine. If anything, the prayers we were saying at that moment were pushing me away from any feeling of fellowship with this group. We were into a section of the book where the prayers were all of the most visceral kind, focused on the Most Blessed Sacrament as the actual flesh-and-blood presence of Jesus.

*Blood of Christ, falling upon the earth in the agony—
save us.*

Blood of Christ, shed profusely in the scourging—save us.

*Blood of Christ, flowing forth in the crowning with
thorns—save us.*

*Blood of Christ, Eucharistic drink and refreshment of
souls.*

Then we were off into another disturbing prayer, something
about "blood and water gushing from our Lord's feet." The
woman who enunciated behind me gave special emphasis to
the "uhhhh" in "gushing" and I felt for a moment that I might
be sick. This was raw God, all right: raw, bloody, and a bit too
much for me.

It wasn't quiet outside the church. It occurred to me that
it had never been quiet, not once in this whole night. Engines
were whining and circling around the shrine, as if downtown
were a racecourse and we were at its center. I felt as if I were
inside a knot that was growing tighter, the chain-saw keening of
the night drivers outside, the density of belief inside. I looked at
the people around me, their prayers almost lost in this racket.
They looked plain, decent, not even slightly ghoulish. How
might I think about all this bloodiness in a different way?

There had always been sacrifices in ancient times—sheep
and goats with their throats slit, virgins thrown into pits—all to
appease gods with roaring appetites and scant mercies. But the
Last Supper and Crucifixion shuffled the players in the sacrifice
ritual. Instead of consuming, God is eaten. God is the meal.

Jesus passes himself around a table and invites his guests to partake. What does it mean to eat God? Doesn't it mean that we are taking the wonder, the radiance, the mystery that we call God into our bodies? And by doing this, don't we become part of God and part God for just a moment, shot through with little sparks of divinity?

I could accept this imagining of the Eucharistic event. I even liked it.

But all that droning on about blood! At the church of my childhood, I don't recall that much attention was paid to Christ's blood, even at the communion. Paper-thin disks of bread were passed out by the priest (the kids used to play at this later with Necco candy wafers), but there was no communal drinking of the wine that had supposedly been transformed into Christ's blood. The Catholics at St. Paul Shrine not only emphasized the communion wine; in this prayer, they were clearly pairing the Eucharist—the two-thousand-year-old echo of a nice Jewish seder—with the host's execution the next day. What did the first incidence of blood have to do with the second? Obviously, both are God's blood, not the blood of human beings, a point that seemed lost on succeeding generations of Crusaders and Inquisitors and other Christian soldiers intent upon killing those who didn't believe what the Church said they should believe. My knowledge of theology is sparse, but from what I know of the New Testament, there was no authorization for that kind of behavior. Certainly, Jesus didn't look down from the cross as the Roman soldiers dug a spear into his side and tell his followers, "Do *that* in memory of me."

So the blood is God's blood, shed, as we are told, for us. A few months after my night vigil, my daughter groaned at the mention of the nuns and asked, "You're not starting to believe all that garbage about Jesus dying for our sins, are you?" Not for our sins, I shot back, the blood prayers still agitating at the back of my mind. I do believe in sin, but I've always had trouble with the idea that we're born with it as a result of bad behavior on the part of the first humans. The Adam and Eve story strikes me as unfair: we are barely to God as my dogs are to me, and I'd never leave so much as an uncovered butter dish within their reach. But the Crucifixion story seems meaningful to me when I look at it another way: that Jesus stepped forward and said, in essence, I will suffer to save you from your own limitations; I will give you an example of someone who chooses suffering to help others; and further, I will face the worst of what all of you will have to experience at some point in your life—betrayal, ridicule, pain, and death—and by doing so know you as well as any creator can. In a sense, he was saying: I will become you. When I began to look at the blood imagery this way, I could see that the Last Supper and Crucifixion stories completed each other. In the former, humanity is invited to become divine. In the latter, the divine becomes one with humanity.

All this meditating on the blood prayers pulled me away from any awareness of the people around me; who knows what they were saying while I was rumbling along with these unfamiliar cogitations? By the time I was aware of the room again, the prayers were very different. I picked up my book in time to read the end of a psalm:

Many say, who will make us happy?
Let the light of thy countenance shine upon us, O Lord!
As soon as I lie down,
I fall asleep in peace,
For Thou alone, O Lord, dost make me dwell in security.

The hour ended with this balmy little prayer, and I padded out to the Guild Room in my socks and had another piece of banana bread. I had taken a slice during each hourly break since it seemed like I needed a little something extra to fortify myself for all this holiness; at that rate, I'd eat ten pieces of cake if I made it through the night. By now, the gatherings in the Guild Room were getting kind of clubby. There was a certain camaraderie developing, a certain triumphant look exchanged as we passed each other on the way to the bathroom or stood around on the church steps to look at the stars. "I can't believe I've made it this far," I told Kim as we met under one of the stained-glass windows, still darkened and dull. "I'm more than halfway there." And then I knew: I'd last the night, staying not only through the vigil but also until Father Senan's last mass at St. Paul Shrine.

I had hoped in vain that he'd change his mind about leaving St. Paul, but this wasn't to be. So I had nailed him the week before the vigil, telling him that we needed to schedule an exit interview. I'm not sure if he was familiar with that particular term from corporate human resources, but he said sure, he'd let me grill him one last time. I came early for our interview and spent fifteen minutes in his living room marveling at the collection of porcelain friars in the china cabinet: salt and pepper shakers, cream and sugar sets, egg cups, all showing chubby, puckish, tonsured friars in brown robes. Did he have a fondness for kitsch, or was he just dutifully displaying gifts from parishioners?

When he arrived, he settled himself in his familiar chair of Catholic tweed, resting his hands on his knees so calmly it was hard to believe he was on the cusp of this great transition. "Fire away," he said. "You have my undivided attention for thirty minutes."

"Are you retiring?" I had heard so many different versions of where he was going next that I wasn't sure he actually had a new destination.

"The only retirement in my order comes from a heart attack or a stroke," he said, sounding amused. He explained that he was going on to be the number-two man in a thriving Charleston parish, and that the senior, a man in his upper eighties, had been his chemistry teacher in the seminary. "It'll be a full house at every mass there," he said, waving his hands in front of his eyes as if dodging a swarm of gnats. "I won't know what to do with all those people!"

He talked a little about the dwindling numbers in his order, but he felt hopeful that this would change. There had been many times in history when the ranks of the religious had fallen, he said, and these times were often followed by periods of resurgence and even the formation of new orders. After World War II, there was an enormous revival, and then there was Vatican II. "Who could have predicted that?" he asked. "We'd been in a rut for five hundred years, but Pope John XXIII created a great wave of change. We're rocking in it still. He was an old pope, and no one thought he'd cause any trouble."

I wondered about this optimism. I've asked others of the religious about their dwindling numbers, and almost all believe that the life of vocation will never disappear. "It will survive," Sister Mary Rose had told me. "It's been around for two thousand years. There were tons of religious in the 1940s and 1950s, but that was an anomaly when you look at the whole of our history. Religious life is like yeast: it is hidden, small, there aren't lots of people involved at any one time." I wondered if this was the kind of thing they have to tell themselves to push away the terror of possibly being the last of their kind.

"Will you miss the Poor Clares?" I asked Father Senan.

"Of course!" he said. "I share the Eucharist with them once a week. It's great to have fifteen women at your feet."

I could imagine how Mother James would laugh at this. "What will you miss the most?"

"I like saying the mass over on their side of the church in the winter. It's dark and quiet, and you can see the dawn coming through their stained-glass windows. And I like going into the church at night, knowing they're over there praying. They're quiet—I can only hear the occasional shuffling of feet or a cough—but I know they're always there."

I was so fond of Father Senan that I could have stayed in his company for hours, following one question with another. He had the kind of silvered brio that only old people have, not that all old people have it; he was marked by a weathered contentment, steadfast kindness, humor, and wisdom. He was someone—and still is, as far as I know—whom I couldn't imagine ever losing his eagerness for life and his capacity for outrage. I was afraid I would miss him terribly and that going to church would lose its appeal without him.

"Here's something I don't get," I told him. "I know that the priest stands in for God at the mass, and that I should be able to have the same experience there whether or not I like the priest. But I don't think I can do that." I pulled out a piece of paper and read him something I had found in an essay by the wonderful essayist and writer of fiction Andre Dubus:

> *I like this priest, but liking him is not important. A priest can be shallow, boring, shy, arrogant, bigoted or mean; during Mass, it is not important. I believe most Catholics go to Mass for the same reason I do: to take part in ritual, and eat the body of Christ. If the priest is an intelligent, humorous and impassioned speaker, then the Mass includes the thrill of being entertained, even spiritually fed. I know that a homily can affect the soul. But a mute priest could perform a beautiful Mass, and anyone could read aloud the prayers and the Gospel and the words of the Consecration of the bread and wine.*

"You were gone once and a boring priest who looked like Ed Wynn took your place," I told him. "I didn't feel the same and I couldn't feel the same."

"The priest is just the one who calls everything together," Father Senan said. "Christ appears in many guises, and that's the difficulty: seeing him in one another. There is the spark of the deity in everyone, no matter who they are. You make a leap of faith when you look for this."

"Oh, yeah, faith," I said, wincing. "That old stumbling block."

"Faith is a gift, sweetheart," Father Senan said, rising to his feet because it was time for him to go. "But it's a gift you have to ask for."

I was pleased when I realized that I was going to make it through the all-night vigil, but when it suddenly occurred to me that we were all counting down the few remaining minutes until Father Senan's last mass I became melancholy. Sometime after 4:00, new people started to arrive looking fresh and clean; the rest of us looked as if we had slept in our clothes—as if we had slept in our *skin*, which was also sagging and crumpled. At 5:40, the server arrived and lit the altar candles. Just before 6:00, Father Senan strode in wearing his brown robes and reemerged at the front of the church a few minutes later, wearing a cape that would have made Elvis proud: white satin with glittering blue flowers. Throughout the night, there had only been one or two of the nuns taking their shifts behind the grate next to the altar; now they all entered, their movements slow, their silence heavy, their faces swollen. When they sang, it was in a minor key. Everyone hung around after mass to say good-bye, but Father Senan took a long time getting back to the lobby. He spent less time chatting than usual; he seemed to take less pleasure in it. There were quick hugs all around, and then he was gone.

He was gone, but many of us who had stayed the night

couldn't seem to leave. We picked at the banana bread, swirled milk in the dense, black coffee, and made groggy conversation. "I heard the birds at three fifteen this morning," Kim said as we watched the daytime traffic begin to dart down the street outside.

"Father Senan used to go out bike riding every morning," I said, recalling part of our last interview. "Not quite when the birds get up and not quite this late, but around five—after the criminals go home but before all the other people start going to work." I had asked him if he wore his robes while he pedaled, had imagined his cord streaming and bouncing behind him. He had laughed and said no, he wore biking shorts and a black-tasseled hat. I am also an early-morning biker and so is my father, and I liked the thought of Father Senan speeding along inner-city streets toward the dawn. I was sure he greeted each day with joy because you almost can't help it if you're outside at that time. It had occurred to me that what I might most like about this church were the people who tended and gathered around it.

Kim was delighted. "Just think of all those homeless people who sleep outside the buildings downtown. They had no idea that he was a holy man. They didn't know he was blessing them as he rode by."

I hadn't really thought about it that way. I had liked the idea of Father Senan passing through the world as just an ordinary guy, enjoying it in an ordinary way; maybe I liked the idea of him riding away from the burdens of being a holy man. But I supposed Kim could have been right. Maybe he had blessed the homeless people lying on their cardboard mats. That was the thing about having faith: you can decide to be good all on your own, without faith, but it seems to me that faith helps you see the goodness in other people—even if it's well hidden. Father Senan might have seen the spark of deity in them, even if they were pissing on the sidewalk and screaming obscenities at the dawn. He might have even whispered that he loved them in passing, just as the fierce old Sister Agnes had when she kissed my hand.

The all-night vigil seemed like a bit of a bust, at least as far as my own spiritual search was concerned. Even though I was pleased that my body still had the resources to stay awake past eleven—these are resources not evident in my ordinary, nonvigilant nights—I was a little disappointed that I hadn't been suffused with a sense of God's presence. I had been half dreading, half yearning for the divine tap on the shoulder, the cosmic come-hither that other people have experienced. When it didn't happen, I was almost huffy: If God was out there, why did he seem to take no interest in me? Then I remembered that my most heartfelt prayer that night had been only to stay awake. Had God decided that if I was going to make such a puny prayer, he'd go ahead and answer it just to teach me a lesson? Was he really such a comedian?

I didn't think that this was the way God operated—after all, that's human behavior. Still, I remembered what Father Senan had said about asking for the gift of faith. "All right," I said a few days after the vigil. "I'm asking now, so would you please give me faith?" I drummed my fingers and tapped my foot and took my spiritual pulse over the next couple of weeks. Do I have it yet? How about now? I tried to remember to pray and went to mass almost every Sunday. I also made an appointment with St. Paul's new pastor in the fall, thinking he might be the one to deliver an explanation of faith.

Father Bob was a Franciscan in his early thirties and was altogether a far less colorful and folksy friar than Father Senan. The change was even evident in the living room, which had been converted to a large office. Gone was the china cabinet with the tonsured salt and pepper friars, gone the Catholic tweeds, gone the frayed rugs and teetering lamps. The walls had been painted a warm peach. There was a new couch by the window, a row of filing cabinets, a computer with a burbling fish screen-saver, and a ridiculously small desk; since there were papers neatly stacked all over the floor, I figured that a larger desk was on its way. When Father Bob entered, he was wearing a polo shirt and dress-casual slacks. He might have even had a touch of mousse in his short-cropped hair. I had met him the Sunday after the vigil and liked him almost immediately: he was friendly, humorous, smart, and amazingly at ease in his new role. I missed Father Senan—I even missed saying that wonderfully musical name—but I knew that I tended to let foolish thoughts of fawns and doves get tangled up in our discussions about faith.

Father Bob whipped through a lot of my standard-issue questions about faith—not in a glib or shallow way, but in a way that showed he had wrangled with them recently. I often had the feeling with Father Senan and the Poor Clares that they had settled these questions so long ago that they couldn't really muster a fresh answer—it was like lifting a rusty old sword—but Father Bob hadn't been worn down. Better yet, he had taught at a seminary for three years and was the ideal person to field spiritual spitballs. I suffered my usual reticence for a few minutes—after all, what if I asked him a question that would make *him* lose his faith? Yes, this was laughably arrogant. So was my surprise that he had answers that didn't make me harrumph.

"Did you get these questions all the time from those young men in the seminary?" I finally asked him. "Is this the kind of stuff you cover in remedial theology?"

He stopped looking professorial and laughed. "These are questions that a lot of people who are struggling with faith ask."

I told him about my clumsy attempts at prayer. Well, I didn't tell him about *all* my clumsy attempts. I didn't tell him about the novena—a prayer said nine times a day for nine days in a row—that I said for my daughter when she and her boyfriend broke up. She seemed to have perked up by the sixth day, and I forgot to complete the cycle. I didn't tell him about my attempts to say fixed-hour prayers, which are a daily routine of prayers patterned on the Divine Office. I couldn't make it for more than a day because I kept forgetting to pray on the correct hour. I was thinking of borrowing my friend Skip's old watch, which plays "Guantanamera" at preprogrammed hours—he saves it to annoy his Rolex-sporting brother-in-law—and using it to summon me to prayer. I didn't tell Father Bob about the compilation of prayers coined by the saints—not only the well-known ones like St. Francis of Assisi or St. Teresa of Avila, but also obscure ones like St. Euplus—that sat by my desk. I kept planning to flag the prayers that moved me with sticky notes. Instead, I did little more than pick up the book from time to time and read the tiny little verse printed on the back: "Lord, help me be a soul of prayer; help me that all my works swim in prayer." I also didn't tell him about the few weeks in which it seemed that prayer just glinted off me. It just happened, it just occurred without my willing it, and then it stopped.

"I have a hard time praying," I told Father Bob. "It's not just that I don't know what to say, but I never seem to remember to do it."

He didn't seem dismayed by this and effected a little nose-and-mouth shrug. "As people discover a need for prayer in their lives, they make a commitment to take the time to do it."

The only time I had ever paid much attention to prayer was when I was a Catholic school kid and my class was routinely marched off to confession—was it once a week? All the kids would huddle after it was over, with lots of "What'd you tell him?" and "What'd he give you?" It was almost a badge of honor when the priest dumped a heavy load of prayers on you: it meant you were *bad*. "I never thought of prayer as much more than punishment," I said.

Father Bob told me that his own prayer life had been formed as a child, through habits urged by his parents: prayer first thing in the morning, prayer at meals, prayer just before bed. "Of course, there were all those things to memorize, but my experience of growing up in faith was mostly relational," he said. "It was about forming a relationship with God. Prayer was the way that you communicated."

"Do you sometimes wish you could spend all your time praying?"

He looked at all the piles of paper on the floor: they were like an army of the temporal world, marshaling him into busyness. "The contemplative life is very hard, but I think everyone desires something of it," he said. "It's been referred to as 'wasting time with God.' It doesn't make sense in the eyes of the world since there's always so much to do. The sisters' mission is somewhat unique: they've been doing it quietly, steadily and without a lot of fanfare for at least seventy years."

At this point, I knew much more than he about the Poor Clares of Perpetual Adoration's history—I probably knew more than most of the nuns themselves did. I knew that this group had been pursuing the contemplative life for many more than seventy years and that they'd started on the other side of the world. The pursuit had been difficult in ways I'd never imagined. It all started with a boy and a girl and their great enduring love—and I was still trying to make sense of this love.

In this particular story, the boy and girl were chaste and pure, even though they traveled the same burning path to share their love with the same infinitely distant yet ever-present spouse. At least, this is what all the various accounts in Jimmy's stack of manuscripts told me when I finally spread them out on my desk: the fat, spiral-bound manuscript written in 1945 called *God's Own Story*; the half-finished version written in the 1970s labeled *Called to Oneness in the Body of Christ*; the slim leather-bound life of the foundress translated from an elegantly handwritten French version, fragrant and tinted with age, attached to the back of the book; and the version by the now-deceased Sister Anne Marie, densely handwritten on the kind of translucent stationery people once used for airmail. There is actually a pile of other half starts and notes, and, in fact, none of the manuscripts is finished; none takes the reader to the time in which the writer was at work. Why so many efforts to start once again at the beginning? Why do all the accounts taper off before the nuns of yore even reach Cleveland?

I think that maybe they were just eager to get the story right. Maybe as the years went by, changes to the way they lived their faith compelled them to reexamine the stories of the boy and the girl and those who came after. Perhaps my little group of Poor Clares are like every family: they can't get enough of their own roots, they're always tapping away the dirt to examine the tiniest fibers of history—the words spoken by this one to a stranger, the illness suffered by another at the beginning of a journey, the tricks someone else used to keep a loved one from moving on. Or maybe the reason they can't finish the story is that they're only fascinated by their early history, that heroic era of great dangers and bold sorties that created their community, and less so in the maintenance era during which it merely endured. In any case, no matter how many times they write about the early days, they never speculate about any sort of feeling between the boy and girl. They're *nuns*, after all—they don't write those kinds of stories and maybe they don't even have those kinds of thoughts. I do, though: just as other writers have speculated about the bond between Francis and Clare, I wonder about John Baptist Heurlaut and Victoire Josephine Bouille-vaux. Can two people share a passion without it leading to flushed cheeks and trembling hands? Isn't there a thread that ties all passions together? I'm not suggesting that John and Josephine weren't as chaste as portrayed; human nature doesn't have to mean that people shuck their principles and rush into their desires. Mother James doesn't cut human nature this kind of slack. When I asked her once how God could expect poor Eve to resist that apple when she was only human, Mother James looked at me with great dismay. "People use that as an excuse for everything," she said, then raised her voice in singsong mockery. " 'I'm only human, I'm *only* human.' " Maybe John and Josephine turned a similar gimlet eye on human weakness. In any case, they didn't let it stand in the way of their vision.

John wasn't just any John: he was Father Heurlaut, a twenty-five-year-old priest in the village of Maizieres-les-Brienne in 1841. The French Revolution had stifled religious activities in France, but by Heurlaut's day the heralds of Catholicism were sounding a resurgence. He was one of the fervent few trying to lead the way, and Maizieres-les-Brienne was his first parish. However, he was in despair: the townspeople were pleasant to him, but they were cheerfully indifferent to the Church. As he prayed in the town's church with its twelfth-century sanctuary and its sixteenth-century stained glass—the bricks and mortar of the old faith—one thought gave him hope. He wanted to found a community of sisters who could teach a girls' school and engage the local women in spiritual activities and thus lead the village back to the Church. But who among these village girls could provide the spiritual spark? One day, the vicar-general pointed out the young and virtuous daughter of the mayor at a village ceremony, and Father Heurlaut felt sure that she was the one.

None of the accounts on this side of the Atlantic say much about Josephine as a young girl, but one thing seems clear both then and throughout her life: she was uncomfortable with the mantle of greatness that the priest wanted to throw across her shoulders. She was helping her aunt with the family's charitable works and wasn't initially interested in the priest's plan. But after many prayers to the Virgin Mary, she believed she got the nod. She acquiesced to Father Heurlaut's dream and went off to boarding school in Troyes to get a teaching certificate.

Here I'm getting caught up in the details of these histories, which are interesting to Jimmy, the nuns, and me, but probably not to anyone else. The details don't yield the kind of drama about the kind of heroes that would interest many people. Some are tediously churchy. Some are trivial: how Josephine was the oldest student at the teacher training school; how the first woman who joined her community became blind; how the community's first home was in a Parisian apartment. I guess the Poor Clare writers clung to these details because that was just about all they had. They were making an earnest attempt to put flesh back on some very dry bones.

At least one of the details is terribly poignant. As she lay dying, Josephine recalled a time when she was a child and went skipping up to a man she mistook for a family friend. Weeping, she told the nuns standing around her deathbed that the man had rebuffed her and that she "felt it so keenly . . . that she attributed to this first wound her exterior coldness which, by those who did not know her, might sometimes be taken for insensibility." Josephine, or Sister Marie Clare of the Franciscan Nuns of the Most Blessed Sacrament, as she was later known, seemed to have been a woman of deep faith but unremitting melancholy. As the little leather-bound book says,

> *God allowed Mother Mary Clare to suffer very acutely from those whom she loved most dearly. In her continual anguish and many heartaches, she always evinced the same equanimity; and whenever a more penetrating eye surmised the Reverend Mother's pain and wished to console her, she answered in terms that proved she desired and expected relief from God alone.*

Poor Josephine. The small book smelled sweet—it left a caramel fragrance on my fingertips—but it seemed to me that her life had little sweetness, even though it had elements of a kind of greatness. The author implies that Josephine was indisposed to happiness, that even when she was a little girl she worried that too much happiness meant "she might not be on the path to heaven whereon she knew God is wont to conduct His elect amidst crosses and tribulations." *How convenient*, I would have once said to myself and anybody else who wanted to listen; what a convenient way for the Church to explain suffering, to repackage it as some kind of heavenly bounty since neither faith nor religion can make it go away. Now I'm not so caustic about the need for a bromide but I can't help but think that Josephine had it all wrong. At least, when I imagine God as a being, I imagine him wishing us well and hoping our hearts grow through our suffering. I don't imagine him inflicting pain upon us, one tribulation after another, as if we were lab rats and he was looking for the point at which we couldn't even manage basic ratlike behavior. It just doesn't feel right to me.

Josephine's suffering didn't win her the steady affection of her sisters. There were many times when the community raged with discontent, and Josephine even resigned as abbess during one of these times. Eucharistic adoration was a trend sweeping Europe at around the time this order was defining itself, and Josephine and company decided that this should be their mission. Still, the community wrangled. Some of the nuns thought they should have active vocations, an especially tempting direction given that benefactors approached them at their poorest with money to lay aside their prayers and take up teaching. But Josephine stuck to the mission of perpetual adoration. She wanted a special focus on prayers of thanksgiving, inspired by the biblical story of Jesus healing a group of lepers, only one of whom came back to thank him. Josephine wanted her nuns to thank God on behalf of all the ingrates. Her problem was that she had vision but not the charisma that created a swell of faithful followers. Her suffering also didn't win her a peaceful death: there she was on her deathbed, still writhing with grief over her weaknesses. It didn't win her much in the way of after-death recognition, either. Even though she inflicted the kind of physical abuse on herself that made some people saints—and there was even a small, quirky almost-miracle associated with her— she seems to be an exceptionally minor figure in Catholic lore, important only to this particular strand of Poor Clares. And even they, in the fat manuscript written during the 1940s, move quickly through the Josephine years and don't even remark upon her death.

In 1856, Josephine opened her first monastery in Troyes. By 1871, her community had opened a second monastery in Cranow, Poland, which was funded by a countess and her friends. This monastery was ill-fated. Other religious orders in the town weren't keen to have newcomers, local Protestants were incensed to have even more Catholics in their midst, and the countess's friends shared an accountant who told them they should make better use of their money. Finally, the countess herself withdrew her financial support and turned them out of the house she had built for them. The nuns drifted to Austria, where they were embraced by the Princess of Lichtenstein.

From there, the history of these nuns develops more narrative zest. Now, they were facing external rather than internal obstacles. Instead of pages devoted to their zigzagging religious quest and mysterious spiritual portents or the many permissions and allowances and approvals they needed from the Church to build their community, the story tells of their fortitude before the impending terror of the First World War. This was the scourge that drove them to find a safe haven in America. The history is also more interesting—to me, at least—because its heroes were still alive when the writers were at work. "We still possess the human treasures who made it possible for us the Divine Treasure in perpetual adoration; we still cherish the companionship of our loved foundress, Mother Mary Agnes," the writers trill. The heroes were able to offer their scribes not only the salt of adventure but also the odd fruits of memory, passed down by the living hands of old women who had risked everything for their faith.

By the second decade of the twentieth century, war was looming. The nuns in Vienna were visited frequently by Duchess Sophie Hohenberg, wife of the Archduke Frans Ferdinand. She whispered her fears through the grates and had the nuns conduct storm novenas—prayers repeated over and over again to "storm" heaven. The nuns began to worry about their own little empire. They had six monasteries in France, Poland, Germany, and Austria, and they worried that their order might be wiped out completely if war raged throughout Europe. They began to dream of America as the next site for expansion. Even so, when Sister Mary Agnes—not the same Sister Agnes still living in the Cleveland monastery—volunteered to go to "the farthest bounds of the earth to find a safe place for my Eucharistic King," her superior balked, unwilling to send any of her nuns across the Atlantic.

Sister Agnes persevered. She received permission to study English. And then one day, Cecilia Kump arrived at the Viennese monastery to put a welcoming face on America. Miss Kump was born in Vienna, emigrated to Chicago, where she worked as a housekeeper, and had returned to Vienna for a visit in 1912. Miss Kump offered to help the nuns expand their mission to America and, within months, announced she had found them benefactors in Chicago. Sister Agnes and an elderly companion, Sister Josepha, petitioned Rome for permission to leave their enclosure for a voyage to America. Permission came quickly, but their abbess's enthusiasm didn't match that of

Rome. When news of the *Titanic* disaster struck, she papered Sister Agnes's bed with lurid pages from the press, hoping to scare her from making the journey. This didn't work, and even the order's poverty didn't hold them back: the Duchess Hohenberg offered to pay for their passage to America. And soon they were off.

Think of two cloistered nuns managing this epic journey! Certainly, they knew how to face monastic vicissitudes—they knew how to maintain silence for hours, they knew how to tolerate cold beds and a range of unpleasant penances, they knew how to keep their minds in prayer despite the flatulence of the sister standing next to them—but did they know how to find a compartment on a train? Apparently not: the first mishap was that Sister Josepha got lost in the station and they missed their train. When they were finally helped to their ship, Sister Agnes found herself having to manage Sister Josepha as if she were a child. The older nun was terrified of the unimaginable expanse of ocean, but the younger nun and other passengers soothed her. Sister Agnes suggested that the waters were a "beautiful mirror of God's greatness," and that worked for a while. But when night fell, the darkness unnerved Sister Josepha again. The ship kept all its lights burning for the first few days to help the passengers acclimate to the blackness of night at sea, but on the fourth night the lights were turned down. Hours later, Sister Josepha sat up in bed and shrieked, "Agnes, Agnes, I am blind, I cannot see anything. Everything is dark." On another night, Sister Josepha woke again and shrieked, "Agnes, Agnes, the ocean is running into our cabin!" The lavatory had spilled while the ship rocked from side to side, soaking the older nun's sheets. Sister Agnes dried her off and switched beds with her. When they finally docked in New York, Sister Agnes strode from the ship and bent down to kiss the American soil as all the other passengers streamed around her. She was the rock of the Franciscan Sisters of the Blessed Sacrament in the New World. Miss Kump's connections in Chicago didn't pan out, but Cleveland's Bishop Schrembs soon heard of the new order and invited them to establish their powerhouse of prayer in his diocese.

Several years after the Poor Clares moved to Cleveland, there was one more intriguing twist in their story. It was summarized on a loose sheet in Jimmy's pile of papers:

> In 1933, a group of Franciscan Nuns of the Most Blessed Sacrament left the Cleveland Cenacle as volunteer missionaries for far-off India. They were followed in 1934 by others of their number. Thus was founded the first perpetual adoration monastery in that land of paganism, whereby Christ's Eucharistic Kingdom might be extended to His benighted but loved children in that unhappy land.

Jimmy had read this paragraph to me during one of our meetings. " 'That land of paganism!' " he repeated indignantly. "Why, they had more of God's spirit in them than most of the people in this country!" Perhaps he was right: the new monastery flourished and the order spread throughout India. There are now eleven monasteries there and only five in the United States. Most of the five struggle with dwindling numbers and aging sisters, and some can't even manage the twenty-four-hour perpetual adoration. A few years ago, Mother James sent an urgent plea to the Indian monasteries, asking if they could spare a few of their sisters to bolster the order's floundering mother ship here in the United States. Since then, there's been a sort of reverse missionary effect as five nuns from India volunteered to come to Cleveland.

I had met with three of these nuns over the past year. Mother James told me that they were too shy to speak to me, but I guess that the others gradually became less nervous after Sister Regina had ventured into the blue parlor. Finally, one of my Friday-morning interviews yielded Sister Aloysius, whom I barely remembered from the day when I walked through the cloister with the newspaper photographer. She was a round-faced woman who smiled almost all the time, tilting her head back so that the small half-moons of her bifocals reflected back at me.

"I didn't want to do this at first because my English is so poor," she said in a voice so soft that I wanted to get up and unplug the clock; even its ticking made it harder for me to hear. "Then Mother told me that you won't put it down the way I say it, that you're a writer and you'll make it sound beautiful."

I was having a hard time understanding. Her accent was even stronger than Sister Regina's—this made sense, since she didn't converse with nearly as many people. My comprehension was time delayed: she'd say something, go on to say something else, then I'd understand the first thing she had said, write that down, and miss the next thing. "I'll do my best," I promised, worried that I wouldn't be able to catch half her story. She leaned her elbows on the ledge and began.

She said she began to be drawn toward this life when she was eight years old. There had been a special feast in her village and a procession in which the priest carried the Blessed Sacrament and men hoisted crosses to their shoulders and boys swung censers that filled the air with incense and young girls threw flowers. Later, she overheard her mother talking to a friend whose son had just become a priest. Her mother looked sad and sighed, saying that she didn't think she was worthy of having one of her children find a religious vocation. Right then, Sister Aloysius began to pray that she might "work in the Lord's vineyard" as a nun someday. She prayed and prayed, even though she knew that most orders required a dowry and that her family wouldn't be able to pay it. Several years later, she heard about a Poor Clares monastery in Dacca—two thousand miles from her home—that was accepting girls even if they didn't have a dowry. Eventually, she and three others from her village were accepted at this monastery. Her parents were happy but cried because they knew they would hardly ever see her again. Her friends cried because they thought she was wasting her life. You will be like a bird in a cage, they told her.

But she was happy at the monastery, even though the life was hard and some of the new girls weren't able to fit in and were sent away. Soon, the community of nuns grew too large for their building in Dacca and the bishop arranged for them to take over a hospital building that another religious community was vacating in Mymensingh. Their life was harder still in Mymensingh. It was lonelier, since there weren't many Catholics in the area. The neighboring Muslims were disturbed that the nuns were unmarried and without the resident authority of a man. Still, they were kind and even asked the nuns to pray for them now and then. One time, after Sister Aloysius became an extern nun, she had to run to the market in the rain. She had wrapped a black shawl around her face to keep from getting wet, and while she was picking over the potatoes at a produce stand she saw a Muslim who had visited the monastery. He did a double take when he saw her veiled face, then said, "Sister— now you look like *my* sister!" Sister Aloysius had to tell me this story several times for me to understand.

When Mother James's plea arrived, the sixty-one-year-old Sister Aloysius was happy to come to America. She had known six of the American Poor Clares at the Dacca monastery, including the two who came in 1933 to found the community. This was not the case with most of the other nuns in Mymensingh. They were afraid of Americans. They had heard that Americans were violent and divorced each other and put their old people in nursing homes. Sister Aloysius told the others not to be afraid, and gradually the idea of immigrating seemed less terrible to them. Still, they wouldn't have been able to send anyone if it hadn't been for the great change within their own ranks.

The Mymensingh monastery itself had faced declining numbers, Sister Aloysius told me. For twenty years, they had no new applicants. The priests were actually discouraging young girls from considering the cloister: if a girl wanted to become a nun, the priests would tell her to go into a teaching or nursing order. So the Poor Clares externs visited parishes and created a nice brochure to attract young girls. They also added special hours of nocturnal adoration, during which the entire community gathered in the middle of the night to pray for new members. "Clearly, it worked," Sister Aloysius said. "We now have the biggest group of novices that we've had in forty-five years: we have fifteen novices and two postulants. Our trust is deepened by this prayer. We got the answer."

"But why wouldn't God just do this anyway?" I asked. "Why did he need to be asked? I would think that he'd want to have more nuns."

This didn't offend her—if anything, her smile grew broader. "The Lord told us, 'ask and you shall receive,'" she said. "My own parents were very poor, but if I asked them for something and they thought it was right, they would try to give it to me. If my earthly father had that kind of compassion, I also think that my heavenly father wouldn't despise my prayers."

I must have screwed my face up for a while. It wasn't possible for me to ponder God's will without being disturbed, even though a sense of divine presence had been growing in me over the past year. This transformation hadn't been sudden or flashy; rather, it was almost as if the molecules of my body were slowly reorienting themselves. It also wasn't a transformation that I knew would last: my interviews with the nuns had given me a framework for wrestling with faith and who knew how I would feel after all the interviews were over? But even when I was brimming with religious fervor, I still couldn't understand a God who wouldn't want someone's mother to recover from an illness, who wouldn't want someone's child to escape the murderer's gun, who wouldn't use his power to make all things right without being asked. I had argued this with others who

said that God gives us free will, and that was fine with me. I figured we should be free to dig our own holes and then struggle
back out of them—but why should we suffer things like ava-
lanches and cystic fibrosis and rapists behind bushes? These
things have nothing to do with our will.

And then there was the concept of God's plan, also a big
problem. If something was in God's plan, I reasoned, then it
would happen. If something wasn't in God's plan, then it
wouldn't—so why bother praying? When some scientists came
up with statistics showing that prayer "works"—they showed
that sick people recover better when people pray for them,
even when they don't know they're the subject of prayer and
don't know the person praying for them—this was material for
even more baffled mulling. Did this have something to do with
the spark of the deity that Father Senan had talked about: Did
everyone have the power of the deity within them, a power that
they could summon and channel in prayer? Was generous, loving prayer like that practiced by the Poor Clares and the people
in the Kansas City study *part* of God's will? Was it possible that
their faith transformed their prayers into an active force?
These thoughts gave me a headache. They reminded me of the
nights that I would lie in bed when I was a little girl and try to
imagine a new color. I knew that other colors existed, that
human eyes could only manage a certain part of the spectrum,
and I'd try to get a picture in my mind of one of those other
unseeable colors. But I was mired in being human. As I fell
asleep, I'd realize that I was only mixing together the colors I
already knew.

The next week, I interviewed another of the Indian nuns, a beautiful young woman named Sister Frances. Her accent was even stronger than that of Sister Aloysius, and I finally gave up asking her to repeat herself and just listened to the melody of her voice. I knew that she was the one who wrote plays for the community and managed their Web site, and I felt that she might have been a good person to answer my questions if only I could have understood her. At the end of our time, she grabbed my hands and told me that she had been praying that I would feel God's love and know Jesus. She promised to continue praying for me every day.

I had started to form a theory about the Indian nuns after I met them and observed new developments at the shrine: the Saturday prayer hour, the all-night vigil, and another night of charismatic prayer that Sister Regina started on Thursdays. If the Poor Clares were like a sacred fire, the Indian sisters seemed its hottest and brightest flames. I had heard from someone with friends among Carmelite monks that such reverse missionaries were bringing older, more traditional practices back into the United States. Could it be that the Indian sisters were bringing about a revival in the Poor Clares' mission? I asked Father Bob in that first meeting with him. Were they creating the new prayer observances that were bringing small handfuls of people back to the shrine?

The answer was no. He told me that the Indian sisters might seem more lively about their faith because most of them were younger than the others, but that they themselves were not the reason for the new prayer observances. Instead, there was a revival of interest throughout the Catholic Church in prayer and the Eucharist, a response to the decades of Vatican II emphasis on the active nature of worship. "Prior to Vatican Two there was a sense that the priest was up there, the sanctuary was up there, all of us sinners were in the pews, and you watched everything that happened," he explained. "The idea from Vatican Two was that the Eucharist is not just something to stare at. It changed the emphasis from that distant celebration to one in which all of us take part as the body of Christ."

"So now things are swinging back to prayer again?"

He nodded. "Many people have missed some of the traditions—the weekly holy hours, the benedictions—that fell by the wayside. But all that never changed here at the shrine. The sisters' constant prayer before the Eucharist was maintained, even in the midst of liturgical changes."

"I see some people at St. Paul who are too young to know anything about pre–Vatican Two worship." It happened once in a while: young men with grunge-band beards, girls with pierced lips peering around the shoulders of the regulars.

"There are some young people who are very interested in traditional expressions of worship," he said. "My only concern is that this is a nostalgia thing. What I hope happens is that when people come in to pray that they will be transformed by the great love our God has for us to go out and reflect that love in caring for our brothers and sisters."

He warmed to his own message and went on to talk about his hopes for the shrine: that it be not just a place for adoration but a center for active compassion. He had already been speaking to some people about involving the congregation in some project to serve the poor outside the church's doors—perhaps housing for single women with children. I'll help, I said immediately. Because the realization had been dawning in me that the mystique of the Poor Clares' robes and silence and history wasn't enough to keep me coming to the shrine. Even my fondness for them and the people gathered around them wasn't enough. I was longing for a church that struggled to apply the moral imperatives of faith to the problems of the world, not just to the sanctity of the solitary human soul. I wanted a church where people were outraged that some people lived in discarded cars and that not enough was being done, where people wanted to debate and do as well as pray, and I sensed that this eager young priest might be the one to bring those people into the shrine.

So there was much to excite me about the shrine as the year 2000 waned. A new priest with imagination and fire, as well as the two new candidates behind the Poor Clares' grates. I could now make out their faces during the mass: Valerie was pale and still, Joanna dark and animated. I could see Mother James, too, but her visage looked a little like what I would imagine for Josephine: sort of tortured and gaunt. I worried that she might be ill, that she was burdened by the ill health of some of the other nuns, that she was grieving the death of one of the older Poor Clares who had been living in a nursing home.

But there is new blood in the cloister, I told myself; soon, Mother James would be flushed and strengthened by this. Joanna looked particularly radiant. As the mass ended and the nuns left their enclosure, she often stopped at the grates for a second to look out into the church. Her eyes were large and dark, and the veil draped around her face as gracefully as a mantilla. She smiled as if she couldn't believe her own remarkable bliss, waved, and then disappeared.

10

*T*here's a yellowed copy of the article I wrote about the Poor Clares for *The Plain Dealer Sunday Magazine* buried in a pile of papers in my office. I dig it out every now and then to reacquaint myself with those early getting-to-know-them days, now nearly five years past. Here's how the article opens:

> *The Poor Clares of Perpetual Adoration pray. They pray on spring mornings so lovely that even the guard dogs in the parking lot down the street are joyful. They pray on summer nights so hot that people all over the city toss and fret in their beds; they pray undistracted by the buzz of cars leaving the baseball park some 30 blocks away, the restive stillness that follows, and the last shrieks of downtown revelry when the bars close at two in the morning. They pray through the fall and into the winter, when the terrazzo floor of their church stings like ice and the wind from Lake Erie hurls cans along the streets outside. They pray every morning under the*

*stained-glass windows in their hidden chapel, their hands
and their books tinted blue and red and gold by the light from
these storied panes; they pray from their monastery's rooftop
garden at night, where they gaze lovingly at the glow of the
city around them. They're praying as you read this, no matter when you read it, because it's their job to cast a night-
and-day mantle of prayer over the world from their tiny
enclave in downtown Cleveland. They'll even pray for you by
name, if you ask, and beseech the Lord on behalf of your
upcoming kidney transplant or your neighbor's faltering
business or your daughter's broken heart.*

How enamored I was with these women! They seemed to me
less like ordinary people than semimagical beings. Not exactly
angels—I've never cared much about angels—but kind of like
the Lady of the Lake and her maidens from Arthurian legend.
Hidden from the rest of the world but witnessing it still, ever
fresh and dewy with otherworldly mists, an enduring force of
goodness in a chaotic and brutish world.

Well, maybe I still feel that way. At least a little.

I had hoped to work my way through this book and
emerge with an understanding of what their lives are like. The
truth is that I really don't know. Even if they had allowed me to
come inside and watch them day and night, I still don't think I
would know. "When I was in the world . . . ," Mother James has
often said to me over the past five years as she's described
something she said or did before she entered the cloister. She
says it in the same way that someone else would talk about
being *in* the mountains or *in* France or *in* Ashtabula, Ohio. The

point is that where they are now isn't *in* the world: their bodies might be in an old monastery on East Fortieth and Euclid in downtown Cleveland, but they actually live in a place called faith. I've been trying to use these women's stories to pin faith down and map it out. But every time I think I have the map spread out neatly before me, parts of it curl up, break apart, or just fade away.

I still don't know, with any sort of day-to-day continuity, where I belong on this map. One day I met with Father Bob to tell him that I wanted to come back to the Catholic Church, but I asked if the Church even wanted someone like me—someone who isn't always sure she believes in God, isn't sure Jesus ever existed or was the son of God or, if so, that he was the *only* son or daughter of God, doesn't think the Pope is infallible, and disagrees with the Church on many of the controversial issues of the day. And the answer was . . . well, not right away. "Keep coming," he said with that so-earnest Ohio face. "Take your time with it. Stay with it." And while I stayed with it, he'd investigate what needed to be done about that gnarly and I think wrongheaded issue of what the Church expects of divorced and remarried Catholics.

So why a Catholic? some friends have asked. Why not be a less-anal Episcopalian or an equally admirable Lutheran; why not a Buddhist or a Taoist? There are a number of reasons, and the first is not terribly profound. The Catholic Church is where I started back when I was a child. Even though it's changed tremendously, it's familiar enough to feel like church—like *my* church. I'm also drawn back to it because it's still probably the greatest moral authority on earth, though, as I said, I don't agree with many of its positions. But I like it that it takes positions, urges certain behaviors and denounces others, still talks about grace and sin and forgiveness and redemption. I'm probably more familiar with the Church's flaws—say, of its oppression of women or its centuries of anti-Semitism, just to pick two from many—than I am its institutional strengths, but it's where I think I belong, or want to belong. I really don't think there's one perfect church for me and maybe not for anyone: we're all square pegs bruising our edges in round holes. I do want to learn more about the world's other great religions—after all, don't they have the same goal of connecting the human to the divine? I want to borrow their wisdom for my own particular elaboration on faith. But all my life, I seem to have chosen mostly Catholics (usually ex) and Jews (usually secular in the extreme) as friends, and I think that's because there's a certain passion behind these two great religious traditions that attracts me. I don't have any desire to convert to Judaism for a variety of reasons, but one is that I wish I could know the intimate dimension of God represented by Jesus.

Now, that's a big problem. Even just saying the name Jesus out loud makes me cringe. So many self-righteous, meanspirited, and even truly evil people have cracked the name of Jesus like a whip that I'm ready to duck every time I hear it. I have a friend who's terribly chagrined because her twenty-year-old son just changed his legal name from Lance to Sapphire. Maybe Jesus should consider a new moniker. Sapphire Christ?

Okay, I'm trying to get over my Jesus aversion. It helps that Father Bob happens to be a marvelous preacher—amazing, a Catholic priest with the rhetorical skills of a Baptist and he's not even Irish! He brings the implications of Jesus alive in a way that no one ever has before, at least not to me. And it helps that Sister Thomas's paintings are all over St. Paul Shrine, showing a Jesus who doesn't look like the pale, squishy European that 100,000 statues are modeled upon. I like the Jesus in her paintings, although I wish she had some in which he was laughing or arguing and not just suffering. I like it that her Jesus looks like a mixture of all the people on earth: his skin is the color of brisk tea and he's a little androgynous, which is just about right. Sometimes when I'm in church, I put my hands together and close my eyes and imagine this Jesus wrapping his hands around mine. He has a warm, welcoming grip like Artemus and luminous eyes like Lynn's. He's as friendly as the cheesecake brothers, he's as angry about the plight of the poor as the man who brings groups of homeless men to the shrine every Sunday, he's as joyful as the woman with the potato-masher-sized cross around her neck.

I can't always put together this patchwork Jesus, can't even buy the whole God package at times. I'll hear the words at mass—the words that I'm saying along with everyone else—and I'll think, "Are you *nuts?*" It's hard working my way back to belief from nonbelief. There's a tremendous chasm between the two, and it's only some inexplicable determination that pushes me to keep making the leap. Logic can pull you away from God but I don't think it can bring you back. At least, I've tried to find a logic for this compulsion and can't find one. Other people's faith and their words for it can't get you there—as Jimmy told me months ago, "To those who believe, no explanation is possible. To those who don't believe, also no explanation is possible." Feeling can't do it either, since I know from the nuns that you don't always feel God's presence even if you believe in it. Visions might help! A friend of mine—a rational, brilliant former dissolute and skeptic—all of a sudden began having visions of Jesus and receiving pointed messages about the spiritual path she must follow. Now there's the fast track to faith.

For me, it takes a combination of things to reach the belief side of the chasm, where I cling from time to time with gnawed and ragged fingernails. One is certainly pattern: the pattern of visiting the nuns, the pattern of weekly mass, and the pattern of prayer when I manage to stick with one. Retreat, which I learned from the nuns: pulling away from the world to enter a cool interior cave that feels very much like the nuns' own shadowed, silent hallways. And then, finally, the tiniest of convictions that God is like a fire burning in the darkness, whether I'm aware of it or not. Faith keeps me turning to that fire over and over . . . for refreshment, for solace, for strength, for the thrilling surprise of its presence. During these moments of belief, there is simply *more* of my life—it's as if the laws of physics have changed and my capacity for presence has expanded.

And still, my hold on faith is tremendously insecure. A few months ago, I went to mass as usual, and it was a great mass. The nuns did, in fact, sing like angels, and Kenny's hymns weren't obscure and dreary as they sometimes are. The people that I wanted to reach out and touch during that post–Vatican II sharing-the-peace thing were near enough to touch. And

Father Bob's sermon was wonderful. It revolved around that New Testament story of the Samaritan woman who goes to the well for water at the same time that Jesus was sitting there, momentarily minus his disciples. He asked the woman for water, despite proscriptions against a Jew speaking to a Samaritan and a man speaking to an unattended woman. But it wasn't merely a human thirst that made Jesus speak, Father Bob said: he had a thirst for intimacy with this human being, an intense longing for communion with her. I loved this sermon. At the benediction near the end of mass, I felt myself lifted for a moment by the priest's upraised hand, and then I started to tear up again, just as I had on my first Ash Wednesday at St. Paul Shrine. This time I knew why I was crying. I was afraid that I might never be able to believe all this, that I might always be at the fringe of this and every congregation. That I might never have the faith to walk in their midst.

So I sniveled for a while in silence, then walked into the Guild Room to say a quick hello before I made my mournful way home. I poured a cup of coffee and joined Lynn and one of the cheesecake brothers, who were deep in conversation. It seemed that a longtime congregant, a very old woman with puffy white hair who tottered up to the front of the church every Sunday, was dying. Lynn had been going to visit her every day after work. She read her passages from the little brown prayer book that she was showing the cheesecake brother, even when it seemed the old woman was only semiconscious. I told Lynn that this was a nice thing for her to do, but she shook her head.

"We're all a bunch of loners at this church," she said. "Lots of us don't have anyone else. We have to stick together."

Then she waved the book at me and said, "Myron gave you one of these, right?"

I shook my head.

"You're sure? He meant to give you one. He must have died before he got around to it."

Then she told me that she was going to find me one of these books, and that I was to use it this way: I was to open it to any page, and the passage on that page was the one God wanted me to read. She handed her book to me and said, "Try it." And I swear that the passage I read had something in it about conversion and even about writers, even though I've never found it again in the prayer book that she gave me several weeks later. In any case, I didn't feel quite so extremely odd and different.

A few weeks later, St. Paul Shrine was in its glory. It was the Saturday of Sister Mary Joseph's formal and final commitment to the community—her Rite of Perpetual Profession of Solemn Vows—and the streets in front of the church were lined with cars. All sorts of people were running down the sidewalk with flowers in their hands; they looked as if they were afraid they wouldn't get to church in time to find a seat. Inside, the shrine gleamed with matrimonial finery: white flowers in bud vases attached to the outside of the pews with white ribbons scrolling to the floor, white satin cloths on the altar, and more white flowers around the tabernacle. There was a touch of gold on the white marble angels around the chancel: each seemed to be holding a gleaming French horn. Sister Joseph's parents stood at the back of the church greeting everyone who came in, and I thought for a minute that she herself would enter from the back of the church, dressed as an ordinary bride. But when the music started, it was a phalanx of servers, priests, and finally the bishop himself who marched in. A woman in my pew who seemed to be a relative passed around tissues as the ceremony began.

Sister Joseph didn't march down the aisle. As the bishop began to ask the ceremonial questions in a voice loud enough for the whole church to hear, she answered in an equally clear voice from behind the grates. There was a slight murmur from the people around me, who may have shared my disappointment that she wasn't going to make one last appearance outside the cloister—that there wasn't one last walk among us, so that we could watch her pass from this world into the other. But that passage had already taken place eight years ago, without crowds and ceremony. On this day, she announced her vow to remain part of the Poor Clares community all the days of her life—a vow the bishop characterized as "an eternal Yes to almighty God"—and then all the people clapped. The bishop took what looked like a flower wreath and thrust it into the nuns' enclosure, and from way back in the church I could see the flowers bobbing on Sister Joseph's head. Cameras flashed from behind the grates.

After the ceremony, there was a gathering up in the Lady Chapel. Everyone streamed up the steps and filled their plates with the hot food served by Sister Regina's Thursday-night prayer group. One of the tables was crowded with Sister Joseph's siblings and their spouses and children, all laughing and chattering at once. I stopped to talk with them, leading in with some sort of bland comment about what a big day this was for their family. They all nodded, but the children and the food and their noisy enjoyment of each other precluded much in the way of conversation.

"She has such a beautiful voice," I said to her younger sister. It was interesting to see, in her, what Sister Joseph would have looked like had she not chosen to be a nun.

"Yeah, I don't know where that came from." The sister turned to her brothers. "You ever hear Diane sing much before?"

They shook their heads.

"It must have been all those Aerosmith concerts she took us to!" the sister said, handing a paper plate to one of the children. "Or Metallica—she loved those loud bands." Had I not hung around for another hour, it would have been easy to think that this day was only a celebration for her family and not a loss. I stayed long enough to help put away the tablecloths and carry the coffee urns to the kitchen, long enough to enter the blue parlor to offer my congratulations to Sister Joseph after the hundreds of other guests had left. By the time I entered, there were only a few people waiting to speak to her. Sister Joseph stood on the other side of the grates, surrounded by gifts and wearing a crown of thorns twined with roses. She looked tired, but she gripped my hand as if I were the first of her guests.

"Oh, Kris," she said. "Thank you so much for coming. We pray for you every day, and for your mother—"

"My mother's fine!"

"We're praying for your father, too, and your brother, the one with the bad back."

I was amazed that she remembered all this, the constellation of needs in my family, and I was going to tell her so. Just then, I noticed that her own family was standing at the door, waiting quietly for their final moment with her. One brother broke away from the rest. His nose reddened with each step and tears streamed down his face and he reached through the bars to wrap his arms around his sister. Everyone else in her family began to sob, and I left them to their joy and their grief.

It will be years before St. Paul Shrine sees another Rite of Perpetual Profession, as both Joanna and Valerie have left the community. One Sunday, I realized I couldn't see Joanna inside the nuns' enclosure. I told myself that she probably just had the flu or a cold. When I didn't see her for several more weeks, I finally asked the all-knowing Lynn what had happened. "She's gone," Lynn said decisively. "It was not the life for her." Not long after that, Valerie also disappeared.

Some weeks later, I visited the church to talk to one of the other nuns and I saw a woman sprawled prostrate on the steps of the chancel. She had a shawl draped around her face, but when she looked up I saw that it was Joanna: there were the same lovely dark eyes, now sorrowful instead of jubilant. I waited for her in the lobby of the shrine, and when she came out she agreed to talk with me about her experience inside the cloister. We had coffee at a bakery in the old Italian neighborhood where I had tried going to church a few times. Joanna had grown up there and was now living down the street with relatives. She was hesitant about saying anything about the Poor Clares, she said; she didn't want to criticize. But she had found cloister life too chilly. Was there really a need for all that silence? She said she had cried herself to sleep at night when she was there, begging God for the strength to obey the community's rules. When this failed, she even argued a little with the other sisters about relaxing some of their injunctions against conviviality. "I am a naturally friendly, good-morning-how-are-you kind of person," she said, adjusting the shawl around her curly dark hair. "I speak to everyone. And I can't be silent about Jesus."

No, I thought, as I listened to Joanna talk on and on and on: she *couldn't* be silent. I realized that Joanna might be too persistently loquacious for just about anyone: after listening to a half-hour monologue about Jesus, I was desperate to leave the bakery. She might look the part of a holy woman with her martyred eyes and shawl—as she talked I was trying out different bakery-based sobriquets for her (Madonna of the Pignola? Madonna of the Vegetable Stromboli?)—but I could see how unsuited she was for a community devoted to silent contemplation.

Mother James confirmed this at our final meeting several months later. "We had to ask her to leave," she said. "The girls have to have the vocation. Some think they do, but if they can't live our life they don't have the vocation."

"And Valerie?"

Mother James replied that Valerie had found their life too confining. Then she sighed deeply. She told me that this is when her faith wavers—not her faith in God, but her faith in the future of her community. She told me that the Poor Clares pray for new members every day, taking heart from Sister Aloysius's story about the Mymensingh monastery that was empty and then refilled after the nuns prayed. Then she pulled out a pile of photographs of Mother Angelica's new church, monastery, and extensive grounds. The pictures—taken by Lynn, who drove Sister Regina down to Alabama to have a look around—showed many groupings of brilliantly smiling nuns: nuns in the kitchen, nuns in the garden, nuns in a gazebo, even nuns leaning over a whitewashed fence to pet horses.

"Look how many young ones they have," Mother James said grimly, slapping down each photo as if it were a tarot card announcing a dismal fate for the Cleveland monastery. "I think things will swing back here. Joseph thinks so, too. She tells me, 'Why would I dedicate my life to a group that's going down the drain?'"

I wanted to get in my last questions about prayer before my contact with the Poor Clares ended—specifically, before they read the draft of this book and realized what a derelict Catholic I really was. I didn't think I had asked Mother James about her own experience with prayer; I couldn't find it in my notes. So I asked her: How do *you* feel when you pray?

She tucked the photos into one of the folds in her habit. "There you go about *feeling* again," she said with a slightly impatient sigh. "I told you before that it's not about feeling. You can't go by what you feel. You have to go by what you know—that God is there, that you're doing your best in all things."

"It's hard for me to pray when I'm not feeling anything but rushed to get on to something else," I pointed out.

The angles of her thin face suddenly shifted, and she chuckled. "When you pray, maybe you should ask for faith *and* feelings. Tell God you want to be in ecstasy all the time."

"Do you feel that your prayers make a difference?" I felt like the one student who just couldn't get it in a remedial faith class.

"Why would we do it if it didn't make a difference?" She looked at me as if I hadn't been listening for the past few years. "Some things are the will of God, no matter how much anyone prays. But some things will only happen through the intercession of prayer. He knows what we need, but he wants us to ask."

"But why does he want us to ask?" I hoped she would help me make a connection between prayer and the story of the Samaritan woman and Jesus at the well. Did God thirst so much for human love that he greeted each supplication as an opportunity to dive into the human soul?

She waved away my question. "And there has to be a balance between good and evil in the world."

I leaned forward. "You think prayers tip the balance toward good?"

"Well, sure, prayers and charity." She seemed surprised that I hadn't figured this out by now.

"What would happen if everyone stopped praying?"

"That won't happen."

"But if it did," I persisted. "If everyone stopped praying, would goodness dry up and evil run rampant?"

"It won't happen," she repeated. Her Boston accent

kicked in, as it always did when she was most emphatic. "That won't ever happen."

I had to ruminate about the balance of good and evil all the way home. Mother James's final comments reminded me of something I had read in Thomas Merton's *The Seven Storey Mountain*, the account of his conversion to Catholicism and eventual ordination as a Trappist monk. At one point in the book, he reflects upon one of the twists and turns in his path toward his vocation and frets about the many long years it took for him to achieve faith. He says,

> *By this time [1939], I should have acquired enough sense to realize that the cause of wars is sin. If I had accepted the gift of sanctity that had been put in my hands when I stood by the font in November 1938, what might have happened in the world? People have no idea what one saint can do: for sanctity is stronger than the whole of hell. The saints are full of Christ in the plenitude of His Kindly and Divine power and they are conscious of it, and they give themselves to Him, that He may exercise His power through their smallest and seemingly most insignificant acts, for the salvation of the world.*

Who knows what Thomas Merton would say if he were alive today, but it seems that he believed then that even one person's prayers—seemingly small and insignificant—can change the world. Perhaps this conviction is what keeps the Poor Clares praying, even as their numbers drop. All through the day, all through the night, they believe they're dropping prayers like tiny bits of gold on the plate of goodness, weighing against the hatred and despair and cruelty piled on the plate dangling on the other side of the fulcrum.

Why not?

I reported this last conversation with Mother James to my friend Mara, as I always do. I knew that she, in turn, would report it to her many friends and coworkers—some of whom are even Christians and Catholics and have never heard about such stuff. How ironic it was that two former atheists, one an errant Catholic and one a secular Jew, were reflecting this beam of faith to so many others.

"So every prayer adds to the balance of goodness?" she asked.

"Not every prayer," I said. "Not, I think, the ones I said in seventh grade asking God to burn down the science classroom so that I wouldn't have to turn in my science project."

"No, probably not that one," she replied. "And not the one when I was driving down Carnegie yesterday and saw the light turn yellow and said, 'God, don't let it turn red!' "

"No, not that kind," I agreed.

"But when I pulled into the parking lot and said a little prayer for myself and all the other people walking from their cars to their job?"

"Or when I heard about Alan and Rita splitting up and I prayed for them and all the other people reeling through that kind of heartbreak?"

We agreed that these would count.

The priest and the nuns at St. Paul Shrine think that

God drew me to the shrine for some kind of purpose—*of course* they would think that, because that's what people like them think. I don't know about feeling drawn, but I do feel fortunate. I remember when I first sat through a mass and looked at all the people around me and wondered if having faith made their lives any easier. I wondered if faith did them any good. But at some point over the last three years, I realized that it was doing *me* good. I felt subtly buoyed and connected and illuminated by this experience. Happier isn't really the right word, because at times it seems that I feel other people's pains more keenly than ever before—that I'm on compassion overload. But in addition to all the other things that I used to do about their pains—try to be a faithful friend, a helpful neighbor, a kind stranger, a respectful critic, and an activist in one way or another—I also try to remember to pray. Sometimes, it seems as if that's the only thing that matters.

And then, there are the many times when I forget. Something will ambush my daily ritual. Travel or illness will disrupt my weekly attendance at mass. I'll be too rushed to take the time to form a prayer when I hear about a new calamity, or I'll be too dispirited to try. Now that I don't talk to the nuns with any regularity, days or even weeks can go by without my remembering to turn to God. And sometimes when I try to reach for God, I have a failure of vision or imagination, which may be other words for faith: I can't see my way to the door in the darkness, I can't glimpse the corona of the divine glinting around the edges of the mundane. When I manage to bring myself back, I'll feel grateful all over again that the Poor Clares keep praying even when I don't. They maintain the fire of prayer, taking turns to tend it and feed it through the dark nights of the soul—mine and yours. We ache for love and compassion, we warm ourselves at the flames but we often forget to add our own tinder. Blessed are these women, for they continue to nourish the blaze.